# A Random Buzzard in Kathmandu

By

Suzanne Link

A Random Buzzard in Kathmandu

Copyright © 2016 by Suzanne Link. All rights reserved.
First Print Edition: August 2016

Cover photo provided by: John Richard
Author photo provided by: Paul Skinner
Cover Design by: Ready, Set, Edit
Formatting by GigaBook Productions

ISBN-13: 978-1536897470
ISBN-10: 1536897477

No part of this book may be reproduced, scanned, or distributed in any printed or electronic form without permission. Please do not participate in or encourage piracy of copyrighted materials in violation of the author's rights. Thank you for respecting the hard work of this author.

## *Dedication*

This book is dedicated to all those cancer has taken.

You left us much too soon, but unlike Icarus; when flying too close to the sun, ***you became sunshine.***

## Dr. Judith Allen – 61, Des Moines, Iowa
July 13, 1953 – August 12, 2014

Judith was a Social Psychologist Professor at Drake University specializing in theories of consciousness, stereotyping & prejudice, and ethnic conflict & peace-making. She was also a respected teacher in both Tai Chi and Qigong, and a dedicated student in her spiritual quests.

Judith is survived by two children and three grandchildren.

## Dr. Kimberly Townsend – 50, Ames, Iowa
May 28, 1965 – May 23, 2016

Kim was a passionate educator and worked as an adjunct instructor at several colleges and universities throughout the country. She had a beautiful voice that she shared as a member of Saint John's Episcopal choir, and she was an active advocate and volunteer.

Kim is survived by her husband and three children.

## Kristin Katich Sumbot – 26, Reno, Nevada
September 15, 1990 – June 13, 2017

Kristin was a gifted artist who received her degree in art education at Brigham Young University. Her passion for art blessed the lives of many as a teacher and artist. Having beaten Leukemia as a teenager, Kristin was strong and determined. She was an inspiration to everyone that knew her. Kristin is survived by her husband and young son, and her large adoring family – especially her precious mother – Leslie.

Kristin and Leslie at Tenzing – Hillary Airport, Lukla, Nepal, October, 2012.

To the **Souls of Sita Air Flight 601**, Kathmandu to Lukla:

On September 28, 2012, you had to turn in your trekking boots too early, but your adventurous spirits live on.

Benjamin Ogden

Vincent Kelly

Darren Kelly

Raymond Eagle

Christopher Davey

Timothy Oaks

Stephen Holding

Wu Quianming

Wu Lin

Wu Hua

Yang Zhihua

Yang Chen

Bijaya Tandukar

Takashi Thapa

Ruja Shakya

Kumar Marshyangdi

Lakpa Noru Sherpa

Deepen Rai

M.K. Tamang

# Contents

Prologue ............................................................................. 1

The Persuasive Mr. Wittmack .......................................... 3

Cancer Sucks ..................................................................... 12

The Best Laid Plans .......................................................... 21

The Doctor and the Wingman .......................................... 31

AK-47s and a Holding Cell ............................................... 37

The Other Side of the World ............................................ 43

Everything Old Is New Again .......................................... 50

Dream Girl ......................................................................... 55

A Living Doll ..................................................................... 60

Is This Bob Seger's Kathmandu? ..................................... 66

I'd Rather Be Doing Stand-Up, Naked ............................ 82

Piece of Cake ..................................................................... 96

It Only Hurts When I'm Conscious ................................. 114

September 28, 2012 ........................................................... 129

This is Nothing Like the Itinerary ................................... 145

No MONKeying Around ................................................... 156

Ala Freakin Bama ............................................................. 167

Blessed Be My Tie-Dyed Underwear ............................... 174

The One They Call Bama is Lost Again ......................... 181

Dr. Boo, the Walmart Greeter of the High Himalaya ............... 192

The Yak Fest ................................................................................ 208

Goodbye to Florence Nightingale ............................................. 224

What Fresh Hell is This? ............................................................ 238

My Most Successful Failure Yet ................................................ 251

It's All Down-hill from Here ...................................................... 262

My Kingdom for a Horse Named Sweet Pea ............................ 273

The Hardest Goodbye ................................................................ 288

Could Somebody Put a Bell on Me? .......................................... 294

The Stank of Sausage Feet and Home Sweet Home ................. 310

# Prologue

# The Hand Smiles Too

Ten days before departure I have a dream ...

I'm in a dimly lit space that feels like a Vaudevillian theatre, except there's no seating. Velvet burgundy curtains form the walls and the stage is empty. I'm surrounded by people, but don't feel crowded by them. I wonder what we're all waiting for and it hits me: I'm expecting someone to roll a mirror onto the stage. Not a reflecting glass, or a fun-house image distorting one. This mirror is going to let me see myself through the eyes of others, maybe these strangers.

    I'm nervous *and* excited.

    Behind me, people stir and when I turn around my eyes are drawn upward to the wooden balcony. A spotlight creates a soft circle on the curtain that brings favor to the lush crimson velvet. I wait for the mirror to appear but instead I see a puffy, white, cartoonish Hand that resembles a slimmed down version of the Hamburger Helper Hand.

Above me the Hand pulls back the curtain and an Asian boy walks into the circle of light. He's about ten-years-old and wearing a traditional embroidered silk Nauru shirt. Without looking down, he stands in peaceful reverence for a time, then turns to his left and walks into the shadows.

As I try to make sense of the boy, the hand draws the curtain back again. This time, an African boy in tribal clothing emerges. He stands silent, respectful and proud, but he never looks at me either. Then he too turns and fades from the light.

I sense I'm about to understand something big and when the curtain opens again, a girl with long dark hair steps from beyond the curtains, and into my dream. She's wearing a simple peach colored sari and she approaches the rail into a radiant spotlight. She looks down and makes big time eye contact with me. Then she smiles at me. I feel a rush of happiness and love that causes my autonomic nervous system to start to wake me.

The Hand asks me, "Have you seen yourself yet?"

My heart answers, "Yes, I am everyone. And we are all the face of God." I bow my face into my hands and cry. I'm overwhelmed by the feeling of *love*.

As the curtain closes, *the Hand smiles too.*

# 1

## The Persuasive Mr. Wittmack

It's 2012. Two years distance me from breast cancer and as my health grows, so does my hair. Just as life hints at a chance for rhythm again, I meet Charlie Wittmack.

I've maintained my therapy practice from the same rented office space for over 17 years in historic Dilworth, near uptown Charlotte, North Carolina. Here, southern mansions have been converted into inviting workspaces; mine feels like a tree house. Wrap-around windows let in sunlight and hundred-year-old oaks provide a canopy of shade, nests for birds, and a playground for squirrels.

There's been a new guy in the building for several months but I've yet to see him. His mail is addressed to …something to do with cancer and the alphabet. I'm curious.

My husband Brad also rents an office in the building and on the afternoon of May 28th I see crutches outside his door. Someone is leaning over a large UPS package addressed to "Charlie Wittmack," and I figure it's the new guy.

The outside of the box reads "Commercial Crepe Maker" so I ask, "Are you a chef?"

He smiles and shakes his head. "No, nothing like that."

At a loss for another explanation I roll the dice with a guess, "So you just *really* like crepes?"

He laughs, "I guess I do. Or maybe I just like the idea of making a lot of big ones at once."

Right on! This dude has a sense of humor. He's about my height at 5'8" and has strawberry blonde hair, bright blue eyes behind understated wire framed glasses, and his current wardrobe consists of khaki shorts and a blue gingham shirt. He looks early 30's and everything about this millennial screams, "I'm a likable guy. You can trust me."

I'm not gullible but indeed, I immediately like and trust Charlie Wittmack.

I'm curious about my new neighbor and invite him into my office. He explains that he twisted his ankle at the Whitewater Rafting Center while running on a trail.

I think to myself, "Oh poor Bubba, apparently you're not meant for the big outdoors. Maybe you should keep it on a treadmill."

He's friendly and the conversation flows easily; we seem to have a lot in common:

His wife had cancer in 2009. *Me too!* In 2009 I kicked breast cancer in the face.

He's Executive Director for a nonprofit organization that deals with cancer. *Me too!* "My most recent charity work was with Team Raising Love and the "Calling All Angels" art auction. Children drew pictures of Angels that artists interpreted in their own mediums." I pull out photographs to show him. "We had the auction at my friend Gaby's place, Shaine Gallery in Myers Park."

I assume he knows that's Charlotte's old-money, high-society part of town, but I don't want to impress him too much, all at once. When he mentions his Grandfather was a past Governor of Iowa, I assume he can handle my little attempt to impress.

I shift to the physical feat I *almost* accomplished last year. I walked 33 of the 39 miles in an Avon Walk for Breast Cancer. I may or may not know what the inside of a "sweeper van" looks like (the vans that follow the route and give rides to those lagging too far behind, or that simply need help).

He relates to my athletic endurance with a little story of his own about how he recently completed "The World Triathlon." My attention strays as I recall the three events in a triathlon – swimming, bicycling, and running. I take an extra beat to recheck the order as his voice fades back in, "And then, (inaudible) …Mt. Everest."

Oh crap, he's changed the subject and I'm clueless. I redirect, "But wait, back to the World Triathlon thingy. I'm sorry, tell me again. What were the three things you did?"

He repeats that he swam the English Channel, bicycled 6,000 miles across Asia, then capped it all off by summiting Mount Everest, for the *second* time in his young life.

I nod and pretend to understand until I have to admit, "I've never heard of the world triathlon."

He lets me off the hook saying, "That's probably because I'm the only person to ever do it. I made it up."

"*I made it up*" explains everything. Yep, this boy ain't one hundred percent right in the head. But otherwise, he's friendly and pleasant, and he seems harmless.

As we continue talking, it quickly becomes clear he is quite sane, and extremely bright. His adventures may be insane as they cluster around *flying* all over the world *trekking* and *summiting.* We're done with commonalities because I'm not even sure what *trekking* is, and *summiting* sounds like something you'd do in Switzerland. But most importantly is the hard and fast fact, **I don't fly**!

I was classically conditioned to fear flying in the late 80's. I was living in Atlanta and working in a sales position that often required air travel. The frequency of flights increased the probability I'd experience some bad weather and negative situations, but I saw every nasty, terrifying air situation possible.

The final nail in my fear of flying happened in 1988 when my plane got struck by lightning, and the *lightning* was the good part. It started out as a routine flight from Atlanta to JFK, until the sky went dark and it began to rain. Somewhere over Pennsylvania, the plane started pitching and shaking from turbulence. A brilliant white light flashed through every window on both sides, followed immediately by a deafening jolt of thunder. I knew we were *waaayy* too close to electricity!

The plane shook and dropped. People screamed. Something exploded beneath me and my feet vibrated. The plane dropped again and the lights blinked. Some people prayed aloud. Others just cried louder. I had such an adrenaline shock I actually yelled, to no one in particular, "What the hell? Make it stop!"

My heart pleaded, "God, You know I don't like to fly, so I'm not fine with this. If *You think* I'm done then I'm done. But *I think* I'm just getting started, so please don't let it end now, and please, please NOT in a plane crash."

The pilot announced that cargo shifted, and we'd have to make a detour landing in Pennsylvania. Within moments we broke through the clouds to Allentown, and yes, I heard Billy Joel too.

Emergency vehicles lined both sides of the runway, but they left unnaturally wide berths. While the fire trucks dutifully took their front line positions, the firemen planned to man their fully extended hoses, from behind ambulances. The first responders didn't want to be in the same *county* when *this* plane landed.

Complete denial harnessed my acute insanity so I accessed less traumatic, more productive thoughts like, "Are we gonna exit on a chute?" and "If we do, how am I gonna keep my skirt down? Oh dear Lord, am I wearing underwear?"

While the landing itself was unremarkable, the plane didn't park anywhere near the small one-story airport. We exited down stairs and were ushered across the tarmac, to the terminal. When I saw three airline baggage handlers standing outside smoking, I made a beeline to them.

I approached casually and inquired, "Hey, what's all this emergency about …?" We all looked at my plane as a stream of people in odd outfits approached it. I continued, "…and why are beekeepers creeping up on the plane?"

The guy with "Supervisor" on his name tag chuckled and said, "That's the Hazmat people."

I stayed calm and mused, "Why would Hazmat be here?"

The young one was excited and exclaimed, "It's bad new no matter what it is. Hazmat's always bad news." The one in management cautioned him, "Danny, you don't need to say that."

The one dressed like Country Boy Eddie moaned, "We ain't never gettin' off on time."

The Supervisor seemed almost apologetic, "Wrong, we'll be done early today. When Hazmat takes over, we're done. We don't unload Hazmat luggage."

"Wait a second." I was strangely calm. "Are we talking about the flight from Atlanta?"

Danny was still into it, "Yeah Atlanta, and when it's Hazmat, you don't even want your luggage back." When he saw the shock on my face he milked it, "Listen, you don't *even* wanna know."

I insisted, "Yes, I do, Danny. I *really do* wanna know. I was on *that flight.*"

The boss looked from the flashing lights to me and pointed to the obvious, "*You* were on *that* flight?"

I pointed back with more enthusiasm, "YES, yes, *that* flight. What the hell's going on? Let's start with Hazmat."

Danny blurted out, "Dad gum! You oughta consider yourself lucky; *everybody* on that plane oughta."

Country Boy Eddie raised a flannel-shirted arm and grazed Danny across the back of his head. His twangy voice threatened, "Shut up, man." He nodded to me and turned to follow his leader. Danny turned to me, "We gotta go, so take care, *ma'am.*" He ran to catch up with the others and I yelled after him, "Hey, wait! Come back! And *don't call me ma'am!*" But they were gone and I had more questions than answers.

It appears the airline may have been transporting something of a combustible nature that under the right extreme circumstances was a problem. When our plane was struck by lightning and fell, cargo became temporarily airborne. There was some sort of reaction when it hit the hull again. So short story made dramatic; six hours later, on a different airplane, and with no luggage, I landed in NYC.

I came to not only hate flying, but to *fear* it with a white hot passion.

Charlie has changed the subject suggesting I might be a good fit for his group's fall trip to Tibet. They're taking cancer survivors to Mt. Kailash, the most sacred mountain in the Buddhist tradition. He describes how the 22,000 ft. high mountain is circumambulated (walked around) rather than climbed. Sages, philosophers, and ordinary people walk the 32 mile sacred circle so they may be cleansed of all earthly sins and reach spiritual freedom.

That sounds like the most fantastic thing ever, but a single thought checks my enthusiasm, "Unless there's a Tibet, USA, it's too far to drive, and *I don't fly.*"

Charlie gives me a booklet filled with stunning photos documenting past trips, as well as information about the nonprofit organization Above + Beyond Cancer (A+BC). I'm curious and scan the pictures at red-lights. As soon as I get home I head straight to the computer and Google Charlie Wittmack.

I'm blown away by ESPN's documentary on Charlie and The World Triathlon, described by the BBC as "the toughest human endurance event ever attempted." I learn that in 2009, Charlie was "Iowan of the Decade" (Des Moines Register) and an attorney that happens to be Counsel and Fellow for The Explorers Club in New York City, an elite club that includes the likes of Sir Edmund Hilary, John Glenn, Charles Lindbergh, and Chuck Yeager.

My search then reveals information about A+BC and Dr. Richard Deming. A+BC is a nonprofit organization that offers cancer survivors adventures that challenge them physically and spiritually while broadening their understanding of global cultures and fostering their personal growth. He's a doctor, or xray specialist in Iowa (or maybe Idaho?), but he works with cancer patients for sure. I don't go much further because by the time I get to him, I'm already sold.

All of the above sounds fantastic, but the blunt reality is that this trip will require a 24 hour flight to Kathmandu in Nepal, which happens to be on the other side of the world. Worse still, we'll have to make the last leg to Tibet on a small commuter-*ish* plane.

I want to be a part of this amazing journey with all my heart. I just don't know if my heart can take it. The bottom line is that I don't fly—anywhere, for any reason—if remotely avoidable. So, a few days later I thank Charlie for his kind consideration, but tell him about my deal-breaker fear. At first, he shrugs it off, but when he realizes I'm serious, he shifts gears and gives me his complete attention. I try to explain an irrational fear to a rational person and I know I sound lame, but he doesn't shame me. Instead, he shares statistics about air travel safety. He explains that the small plane ride from Kathmandu to Tibet isn't bad and I'm quoting him, "…because at least we aren't flying into *Lukla*. That's *the world's most dangerous airport.*"

He describes Lukla's ridiculously short and steep runway – 1,500 ft. long by 66' wide, with a 15% incline. "It's between a mountain and a cliff and yes, it's dangerous. When a plane crashes, usually no one survives."

He shares a story about a client who heard about Lukla during his flight to Kathmandu and decided to cancel his entire expedition. Charlie, already in Lukla, flew back to Kathmandu to provide a personal escort for his client. He repeats the reassuring statistics he gave his client about planes, mountains, high altitude, and planes in high altitudes in mountains. His client calmed down and flew into Lukla with no problems.

So, according to Charlie, I'm completely and unequivocally safe because we won't be flying into the most dangerous airport in the world. The implication is clear, "Outside of flying to Lukla, all other air travel in the world is *completely* safe."

He's confident and reassuring and I feel silly for being afraid. The experience would surely be worth the risk, so along with hundreds of other applicants, I submit my application. I want to be one of the 15 cancer survivors to journey to remote Mt. Kailash, in faraway Tibet because now, like Charlie's client, I'm ready to board any flight to anywhere, with the persuasive Mr. Wittmack

# 2

# Cancer Sucks

Being diagnosed with breast cancer was shocking. I ended up with two surgeries, six rounds of "big guns" chemotherapy, 33 rounds of radiation, an infected power port, and a blood clot in my neck. I had ticks *and* fleas.

It started on a hot June morning in 2009, during my annual mammogram. Actually, I was six months late making the appointment, but I was only 44-years-old. It seemed like a lot more x-rays were being taken than in past visits, but I surmised it was due to a change policies or procedures. After the first set of pictures the tech was instructed to take a second round. I wondered if maybe she was new at her job. By the end of the third set I'd concluded, "It's probably *me*, not her."

As she escorted me back to the lobby she spoke softly, "You know, *Hon*, we call about ten percent of women back, for further (whispers) *testing*."

She didn't stop walking so neither did I, but I let her know, "*No, no*, I didn't know that. Do you tell everyone you call ten percent back?"

She was sweet to the point of adopting a child's voice, "*Nooo Honey, nooo.* Just the ten percent with, (whispers) *tumors.* Now don't you melt in this heat O.K.? Bye-bye."

I was taken off-guard, but I didn't freak-out. My gauge as to what's scary or risky was probably mis-set in childhood. I tend not to be the freak-out type.

I grew up a country kid in a small southern college town. Tuscaloosa, Alabama is the home of the University of Alabama Crimson Tide. The legendary football coach Paul "Bear" Bryant could have easily been governor, and the current coach Nick Saban, well he's worshiped by all the local denominations.

As a young child, I rode motorcycles, go-karts, lawn mowers, and tractors with my brother and cousins. We rode on trucks with legs dangling off tailgates or stood behind the cabs while barreling down bumpy, potholed roads. The road that separated our house from our cousins ends in Lake Tuscaloosa where we went fishing and swimming, often without parental supervision. My cousin and I joke that our parents played fast and loose with our safety, but the truth is, they were country kids, who were from country kids, who were from country kids.

I was raised around relatives on my maternal Grandmother's land. She gave her three children land on which they built their own houses around hers. I nicknamed her Mu – pronounced moo because of the mumu dresses she wore in the seventies. My Grandfather was nicknamed Turtle because he was a part-time Alabama State Trooper with a lead foot. He taught all his grandchildren to drive his truck before we could reach the pedals. We'd sit in his lap and drive through corn fields learning to change gears using the stick shift on the steering wheel.

When my brother, cousins, or I got in trouble, we had to answer in Mu's Kangaroo Court. She was the Judge, but Turtle was our Defense Attorney. My Grandparent's home was a safe and loving place that I often retreated to when things in my own home got scary.

After the mammogram, I paced on my deck and let it sink in. *I have cancer.* God and I have had our own *on-again, off-again* phases, but we've always been passionate about each other even though I'm the only one with the temper.

I prayed in earnest, "I don't know how to do this, this disease, this **cancer**. Please help me role model to my child in ways that will keep Emma safe from the emotional and spiritual pain that can come with something like this. Amen."

Emma, 14, from the second of my three marriages, walked outside and asked, "What's wrong Mama?"

I got the words out, "It looks like I have a little bit of breast cancer."

She wrapped her arms around me and uttered assurances, "Oh, Mama. It's going to be O.K."

Standing under the warm June sun, I hugged Emma for the longest time since she was two. Emma Claire greeted her life a full month early, attached to the biggest umbilical cord the doctor had ever seen. She was too eager to wait four more weeks because *she* was ready. She's a lot like me, and then again, very different. She's fiercely independent, opinionated, and a little smart-mouthed. She's also beautiful, intelligent, funny, and highly creative, but those characteristics probably come from rogue genes on her Dad's side.

I released her from the hug, not wanting to push my luck. "Yes, of course it's going to be O.K. It's *already* O.K." I excused myself to the bathroom and within minutes, Emma was there with red eyes, a tissue, and ton of statistics on how to *beat* breast cancer. She was taking charge of her thoughts and feelings, and focusing on the solution. I was extremely proud of my girl.

The radiologist called in the afternoon and when he described the size, shape, color, or maybe density, it was clear he thought it was a tumor. The needle biopsy happened the next day and I got confirmation, *I have cancer.*

The same afternoon I got a call from my gynecologist with choices for a surgeon. I picked the one that operated on his wife when she went through breast cancer. He'd been down this hard road with someone he loves very much, and his level of compassion was enormous.

Before we hung up he asked, "Do you mind if I say a prayer?"

I was blown away, "yes …*please do.*" His earnest prayer moved me to tears and I trusted *all is well,* a little bit more.

Within a week I met the surgeon Dr. Turk, and found out he's the best of friends with my Mom's minister, in Tuscaloosa, Alabama. Her minister has prayed with her many times. She's a strong woman of unwavering faith.

She summoned many prayer warriors on my behalf, including my step-dad Arnold. Mom began dating him when I was thirteen, and I wished he'd been my Dad. I began introducing him as "Dad" years ago because I have a daughter's love and respect for him.

At the end of the surgical consult, Dr. Turk offered two choices for an oncologist: "One is absolutely great and has a tremendous personality. The other is brilliant, but doesn't have a great bedside manner."

This choice seems an important one

It was a no brainer and I told him so, "I get unconditional love from my dogs, so it's – *Cocky brilliant bastard* – final answer!"

Turns out, he's been the oncologist for high-profile professional athletes in Charlotte. They all made their cancer battles public, but unfortunately Carolina Panthers Sam Mills and Mark Fields aren't still here to vouch for their Dr.

Until that point the whole process had been at lightning speed, but I'd have to wait three weeks for surgery. Three weeks is entirely too long when there's bad ju-ju in your body. I wanted that crap out *yesterday*.

The first week I spent wrapping my head around my life's latest plot twist. In the second week, I was more than ready to get it over with. By the third week, it was prayer, meditation, and wine …not necessarily in that order.

By time of the surgery I'm sufficiently wound-up to the point I need a large tranquilizer. That morning we had to be at the hospital early and I was ok with that. The sooner I got checked in, the sooner I'd get some sort of anti-anxiety medication.

I love how thoughtful nurses are to make sure you feel calm before surgery. It makes sense though. The calmer the patient is going in, the less likely they are to have problems during and after surgery.

Soon after I checked in Dr. Turk entered my room and introduced his surgical resident, a young guy from Tuscaloosa, last name Nunnley. When my Mom asked if he's kin to a Dr. Nunnley from Tuscaloosa, he perked up, "Yes, that's my Dad!"

In her role as a Vocational Rehabilitation Counselor for the State of Alabama, she'd worked often with the senior Dr.

Nunnley. She was happy to tell his son how much she liked and respected his father.

When he finally looked back at me I smiled and gave him a "Roll Tide," but he shook his head. "Nope, sorry. I went to Auburn."

My response isn't a question, "So you didn't grow up in Tuscaloosa."

He understands where I'm going and makes me work. "I did grow up there. I graduated from the Academy."

Now I know he's local because he referred to the top private school Tuscaloosa Academy, as – the Academy. "I don't understand what happened. Why would you take medical classes from a veterinarian school?"

He continued to swagger Joe Cool, "Because it's the *best*." He pointed at my legs as his index finger queried left and right, "Remind me again, which one of these are we working on today?"

I responded, "Oh this is perfect. An Auburn medical student that thinks he's funny."

He was quick, "No, no …'an Auburn medical *Resident* that's funny.'"

I was as quick, "No, 'that *thinks* he's funny.'" I looked at Dr. Turk, "Seriously, you got anybody besides "*Aubie Jr.*?" – Auburn's tiger mascot.

Funny-boy took exception, "Well I'd rather be operated on by Aubie than by "*Big Al*," – Alabama's elephant mascot.

Dr. Turk corrected both of us, "You're in the best possible hands, because you're getting operated on by a '*Hoosier*.'"

Our bickering stopped the instant a common, and clearly inferior enemy, showed himself. Dr. Nunnley Jr. chided, "Indiana University *doesn't even have* a mascot."

I backed my new ally, "And seriously dude, a *Hoosier* isn't even a *thing*. It's a *non*-thing."

I heard a supportive echo, "It's a *nooothing*."

Dr. Turk laughed, then paused, then became serious, "We're going to remove the tumor and say a prayer before we send it to the lab. We'll get the results back quickly, and hopefully we can stitch you up and be done. If not, the cancer has spread into your lymph nodes you'll wake up with a drainage tube under your right arm. A drainage tube means you'll have to have radiation *and* chemotherapy. We don't want you to wake up with a tube."

Aubie and Big Al agreed to meet in the operating room shortly, after Aubie promised to stand watch against the Hoosier.

I lost track of time for a while but I was pretty sure someone was calling my name. The voice was a million miles away, but someone was breaking the rules and touching my arm – I *HATE* being touched when I'm in any kind of pain – physical, psychological, emotional; don't *touch*, *talk*, or *look*, at me.

A blurry nurse bent over me. I looked at the right side of my gown. I didn't see anything and whispered, "I don't have a tube."

The nurse winced as she broke the news, "No dear, *you do*. It's under your gown."

I knew right then and there, "I'll have to do this thing the hard way, so let's **Roll Tide Roll!**"

I had another surgery because Dr. Turk didn't feel the tissue margins were clear of cancer cells – he wanted *clean margins*. At the same time, a "power port" was installed beneath the skin on my chest to create a constant connection for IV. The port would eliminate repeated needle sticks.

My surgical follow-up was on July 23rd, my 45th birthday. I didn't want to be late to the appointment because I'd get all my lab results. But, in addition to the usual search for phone and keys, I also now had to find body parts. The questions I'd become forced to ask took a toll on my femininity – questions like, "Has anyone seen my hair? Can someone help me find my boob?"

At the examination Dr. Turk reported that he removed the tumor, but also three other small ones. As a result, he had to remove much more of the breast than anticipated. I'd need future reconstructive surgery to increase the size of the right breast, and bring it back into the same zip code as the left one.

But then he gave me fantastic news – my labs looked great, and the tissues around the tumors were clear!

Afterward, I walked into the hallway and bumped into one staff member, took another step and bumped into yet another. It seemed everyone in the office had a reason to be around the checkout counter, so I repeated "excuse me" several times.

Out of place, Dr. Turk's nurse stood behind the check-out counter wearing an unusually wide Cheshire cat grin. I wondered where the receptionist was, but I was especially curious to know what was wrong with Turk's nurse. Looking around I became more and more disconcerted. *Everyone* was looking at me and smiling.

My first thought was dark, "Oh no! Dr. Turk lied to me and I'm dying, and they're all here out of pity and ..." My downward spiral halted when a vase filled with two dozen gorgeous, gigantic roses, was pushed in front of me. I recognized the roses immediately; my absolute favorite, "Texas Big Fun." Yellow and pink petals danced together to create a fabulous tie-dyed effect. The arrangement was hypnotic and stunning.

The nurse gushed, "There's *somebody* here that loves you very much and wanted you to have a reason to smile, no matter what the results; Happy Birthday!"

I heard a chorus of ooohs and aahs and I couldn't help myself, "This is the sweetest thing I've ever seen, and I really like Dr. Turk too, but it's not love for me yet. Tell him we can take it slow and see." Amid laughs and high fives, I hugged Brad and whispered, "Aww, thank you, Honey. Texas Big Fun. *Well done.*"

I began chemotherapy in early August, relieved I liked my oncologist. Yes he was arrogant, but it wasn't a turn-off. Brad often accompanied me and the three of us talked about music, photography, and their favorite, the latest technology. Medicine occasionally came up and when it did, I trusted the cock of the walk.

Treatment, basically a cocktail of poisons injected to kill cancer cells, was indiscriminate and attacked all cells, even the healthy ones. The side effects knocked me on my butt. Nausea was predominant but when I could eat, everything tasted like metal. The absence of hair challenged my body to maintain a consistent body temperature. I was constantly rotating from cap to bald, bald to scarf, scarf to wig, and so on. Hot flashes exploded often. Restless leg syndrome – twitching sensations in my legs – compelled me to strike my legs to stop the jerking feelings. My efforts elicited nothing more than bruising.

Cancer was a wake-up call. I'd never felt vulnerable or fearful for my own well-being, and nothing ever snuck up on me. Yet when it did, I was pummeled by the terrifying thought …"*Maybe I'm not invincible.*"

# 3

# The Best Laid Plans

Typically, I'm only superstitious when it comes to sports. But when it comes to sports, I'm superstitiously typical. Above + Beyond Cancer was supposed to announce in June who's going to Tibet, and when that date comes and goes, Brad feels sad for me. A few weeks later, he's heartbroken for me. At the beginning of July, Brad wants me to accept that I didn't make the cut. But I can't.

I poured my heart and soul into my application and it was solid. Under the section "Advocacy" I described the various fundraising projects I'd spear-headed, and the speaking engagements I'd done. I included brochures from fundraisers and an audio file of one of my speeches. I believed I was a highly qualified candidate and besides, I didn't feel *not* invited, so I sent Charlie an email – something to the effect of, "Respectfully dude, if not me, why not me? And if there alternates, can I be one? If so, how healthy are those ahead of me?"

Brad texts me Monday morning from his office, "Charlie's here." He hasn't replied to my email, so I request a directive, "Go ask Charlie, what the hell?"

Brad states flatly, "Yeah, I'm not gonna do that."

"O.K., I'll text and ask him why not me. No, I'll do better; I'll come knock on his door and let him tell me to my loser face why I didn't make the cut."

Brad throws Charlie under the bus by encouraging me, "Well he's here now, so you'd better come on if you want to talk to him."

"Stop him if he tries to leave."

"No, I'm not gonna do that either."

"Then wait outside his door and if he opens it, stall him – maybe knock stuff out of his hands."

"What's wrong with you? I'm not doing *any* of that."

"Thant's fine. You have your own methods. Just keep him conscious until I get there."

Brad keeps me grounded, "You're not as funny as you think you are."

"*Wrong, Bubba.* I'm *exactly* as funny as I think I am."

Now may be a good time to admit that my sense of humor is *occasionally* impolite. I laugh at the most inappropriate things, at the most inappropriate times. "Inappropriate Laughter Syndrome (ILS)" is the diagnosis I invented. Its purpose is to give me an excuse for being an asshole when someone embarrasses themselves horribly and I can't stop laughing.

Unfortunately, no one's exempt because ILS is *not* a voluntary reaction. I don't pick and choose who triggers an episode, but if you trip and fall in front of me, I'm probably going to laugh. If you do it in a church or a theatre, I may *guffaw*. But if laughter is *the most inappropriate reaction on the face of the earth*, I'm definitely going to pee myself.

Episodes of ILS rarely make me look compassionate, so I consistently try to even-out my edges. Every year or so I take a new class to better myself. I've taken painting classes from different artists, and the class I took from Queens College on Vibrational Healing and Ayurvedic Medicine was a favorite.

By 2008 I'd done enough soul searching and exploration that I'd narrowed my fears in life to two: flying and public speaking. Conquering fear of flying involves an inflexible learning curve, so that fear became accepted as a permanent one.

Instead, I focused on my second biggest fear, that of *public speaking*. I imagined Stand-up Comedy to be the absolute most terrifying platform possible, so logically, I enrolled in a comedy class through *The Comedy Zone*.

A lot of people think I'm funny, so I hoped it would come naturally. It did *not*. There's nothing spontaneous about stand-up comedy, so there's nothing natural about it either. We had to write our own material using formulas and rules. Then we had to *perform* it. I can testify I'm not a good actor; I'm not even a bad one. Worse still, my personality doesn't lend itself to rehearsal. I tend to operate on a *just in time basis*.

At the graduation ceremony I gave an example of ILS from my first wedding. It went something like …

In the spring of 1986, I graduated from the University of Alabama at Birmingham and moved to Charlotte, NC for my first job. There, I met the blond, blue-eyed, athletic and beautiful Randal. He worked for Arnold Palmer building golf courses, and was completing the TPC course Piper Glen.

Randal was from a small town south of Detroit where he'd been a giant fish in a small pond. He was the QB, Homecoming King, and the most popular guy in a large high school. Afterward, he attended college on a full football scholarship.

We got married in the spring of 1987 at my hometown church in Alabama. We decided to write our own vows and to keep it romantic, we didn't share them before the ceremony. Facing my groom, I went first. I may have been a tad nervous, but I kept it together.

Then it was his turn. He started to speak but paused. His eyes widened as his grip tightened and I realized, "Oh, no, he's forgotten his vows and he wants me to help him. But I don't have a clue what they are." At that moment, the first symptoms of ILS encroached, but I held my breath. He began hesitantly, "Suzanne, you're my best friend and I love you with all my heart."

Aww that was so sweet; a perfect start. It was also the perfect place to stop, but he didn't.

He squinted his eyes almost shut as he tilted his head into a question mark, "Our Father, who art in heaven."

What? He's saying the Lord's Prayer! I grind my lips together and fold them into my mouth.

Another pause and the air grew thick. He continued, "Forgive us our debt and don't tempt ... *our daily bread?*"

I still wasn't making a sound, but I couldn't stop my shoulders from shaking. I was a flume on Splash Mountain: I was coming in fast with no brakes, and about to spray everywhere."

The next time he spoke he was barely audible, "And to the Republic for which it stands?"

My mother leaned to her right to catch my attention. I knew I'd better not laugh, but when I looked back at Randal, he was nearly cross-eyed. I lost it and exhaled like a whoopee cushion. A lot of Randal's college friends had come down from

Michigan to celebrate his southern wedding and they thought it was hysterical.

He turned toward them and raised both arms, indicating a touchdown. He finished, "And liberty and justice for all, amen!" My boy fumbled, got sacked *and* intercepted, but he acted like he just won the Heisman!

True stories are the funniest and I got a standing ovation at the end of my "performance." I was thrilled to have conquered fear of public speaking, and equally content to accept my last fear (of flying), as permanent.

Hanging up the phone I repeat to Brad, "I'm coming to the office. Don't let Charlie leave!"

Before closing my iPad I see an email from Above + Beyond Cancer with the tagline, "Join us in Tibet!" I scream, and then a little louder, and then a little longer, and then, I burst out crying. Wait a minute *Happiness*, you're out of your league here. This is *Euphoria*!

On the 20 minute drive to the office I listen to Bob Seger's *Katmandu* on replay. When I arrive I tell everybody in the building, "I'm gonna need about 60 seconds to play a song loud enough for Charlie Wittmack to hear." Brad turns up the volume from his office and Bob Seger belts, "I think I'm going to Katmandu. That's really, really where I'm going to. If I ever get out of here, that's what I'm gonna do."

There's no response from Charlie but I know he's in there. His car is outside and I can hear him moving around.

I motion for Brad to turn up the volume and Seger *owns* it, "K, K, K, K, K, K, Katmandu. I think it's really where I'm going to!"

He opens the door and I yell right in his face, "I got the email Charlie! *I'm joining y'all in Tibet!* Hey Brad, you turn down the music." After a hug and congratulations I confess, "So anyway, I'm relieved. I couldn't understand why *not me*."

He seems confused so I clarify, "I'm talking about my email from Friday." He hasn't read it yet so I drop it, "Never mind, not important, don't bother." I find out they've been sending email updates to the wrong email address.

As days go by reality sinks in and anxiety and self-doubt creep up. I've committed to flying to the other side of the earth and it's starting to make me queasy and dizzy. When I was pregnant, I had a sharp increase in flying nightmares in which planes had to take off on short, narrow city streets, then navigate through skyscrapers and powerlines to get to an ocean. The dreams never ended in crashes but they were distressing, and just one more reason *not* to fly.

I've started having bad dreams again so to help me keep it together, I reach out to my best friend Martha.

Martha and I started our private practices together in 1995, in the same office I'm in today. Unfortunately her husband Phil got transferred to Michigan and I had to go solo. Martha knows me better than anyone and I trust her 100%. I'm positive nothing gets past her so when she accepts the responsibility to vet all information and let me know what to expect and prepare for, I relax. I need someone like her at the helm because red flags are already appearing.

The first flag comes in the form of a *complete change* in itinerary. China's conflict with Tibet causes our trekking passes to be canceled. So now, instead of circumambulating the Kora of Mt. Kailash in Tibet, we're going to summit the 20,300 ft. Imja Tse (Island Peak) in Nepal. A+BC is calling it "A Spiritual Journey of the High Himalaya."

I glance at the new itinerary and imagine it's a piece of cake because it includes the words "Optional Day" a couple of times. It'll probably be like a walk in the park while chatting about, and with, God.

Martha informs me of a whole new challenge—**altitude**. She's researched it thoroughly and wants me to know what she knows. She assures me I don't have to remember *all* of it. "O.K. so oxygen is inhaled through your lungs into your bloodstream, then it goes to your brain and heart. There's less oxygen the higher up you go; the air is thinner."

"Yeah, I've heard about thin air. What does that mean exactly?"

Martha laughs, "I knew you'd ask. The article didn't say, but I wonder too."

"Forget about it, I was just curious." I hear her striking the keyboard.

"O.K., it says, "Altitude is considered to be between 5,000 ft. and 11,500 ft. (1,524 and 3,505 m) above sea level. The highest mountain in the U.S. is Denali in Alaska. I think the highest one in North America is ...never mind, none of this is relevant."

I cut in, "Don't make me use the "t" word (tangential). Remember, your job is to ferret the relevant." I want information strictly on a *need-to-know* basis.

She's as impatient as me, "I know, but listen. Crap, I lost my place."

"That's a shame because we're out of time. But hey, this is a good stopping place for me anyway."

She doesn't let it go, "Here it is. This is what I want you to hear. This is what's important; are you listening?"

"Listening here boss."

"'Higher elevations equal fewer oxygen molecules, so the air is thinner.' Damn it, that doesn't help does it?"

I reassure her, "I'll be fine I promise. And thanks for the riveting synopsis."

She reassures me, "I know you'll be great, *absolutely*. You'll acclimate just fine, *unless you* **don't**."

"Seriously Martha. *Unless I don't?*"

"Well you need to know the symptoms for *if you don't*, just in case."

"I'm not sure I wanna know. I'm sticking with the whole ignorance is bliss thing, so yeah, I'm sure. I don't wanna know."

"Nope, because this part is relevant. Altitude sickness can hit you in one of two ways; your brain or your lungs. Just remember these two acronyms. **HAPE** is High Altitude **P**ulmonary **E**dema. It means you have *fluid on your lungs,* and feels like bricks on your chest. Not like the happy lead blanket they put on you at the dentist office for x-rays."

"Those feel so good. I want one to sleep under."

"Do they sell them? O.K., that's the HAPE one. The other one is **HACE**. That's High Altitude Cerebral Edema; that's when there's *fluid on your* **brain**. It feels like a vice-grip on your skull. These are both very, *very* bad, and I'm just saying, because they could *totally* happen."

The second red flag lands on my doorstep in a package that contains an ice pick, crampons (ice pick shoes), and a body harness. I put a temporary halt on blissful ignorance and call Martha to enquire about the sharp instruments. She's uncomfortable and starts laughing, "I'm not sure." She laughs louder, "But I'm pretty sure, *you need to train a whole lot harder.*"

My training has consisted of hiking, biking, swimming, and walking. I know I'm not *hike-hard* ready, so in addition to her responsibilities to vet all information and relay to me only the essential, Martha adds the role of "training coach." She takes charge of my training and I spend ten of the last thirteen days before departure, in Michigan with her and Phil.

The third red flag hits with hurricane warnings – Charlie has malaria and pneumonia and won't be able to go. This new development is NOT fine with me as he's the only person I know, and that whole "World Tri" thing makes him my safe person.

I give Martha the bad news, but instead of freaking-out with me, she stays calm. I'm in high alert mode but she's not even asking questions. Then I realize she's not upset because she already knows; Charlie Wittmack has been side-lined. When I confront her, she moves quickly, "I'm sorry. Brad and I couldn't decide if it'd freak you out or not. Don't be mad. *Are you mad*?"

"Whoa, Brad too?"

"And maybe Phil."

"*Et tu, Phil*?"

"Well not so much *Phil*. But don't get mad at Brad either. He knew because of some guy in your building that's friends with Charlie. You're already having anxiety and we agreed, you'd find out soon enough. Don't be mad. *Are you mad*?"

I've entrusted Martha as the ultimate gate-keeper of information so that I can keep my crazy harnessed. I trust her intentions and judgement, so no, I'm not upset. But what am I supposed to do now? I've already told everybody and their brother, I'm going.

I hear my Grandmother Mu call my nickname, "*Floss*, you're only as good as your word. If you tell somebody you're gonna do something, you'd best do it or have a humdinger reason not to." I still do what my Grandmother tells me, so against all instinct and intuition, against all the flares sent out by the Universe, and probably, against all odds, *I'm all in.*

# 4

## The Doctor and the Wingman

*(A Doctor and a Priest Walk into a Bar)*

Saturday, September 22, I depart Charlotte at 4:30 p.m. and arrive in Detroit two hours later. As I near the next departure gate I see a group of red Above + Beyond Cancer t-shirts. One of them approaches me and I recognize the man wearing it. I want to make a good first impression on him; I want him to like me.

In the last few weeks I've research this man and learned that in addition to being the founder of A+BC, Dr. Richard Deming is the Director of Mercy Cancer Center in Des Moines, *Iowa*, and a practicing radiation oncologist. Like Charlie Wittmack, he's incredible and far above average in thought and deed. From my perspective, they're both what I call, *"bell-curve fringe."*

Dr. Deming greets me with a wide smile and hug and I notice we're about the same height at 5'8" tall. He's fit with short brown hair and sincere smiling eyes. He introduces himself to me in his best Southern accent, exaggerating his vowels, "You muuust be Suzaaaanne."

Hahaha, he's funny. We're above the Mason-Dixon Line so I admit, I'm the one with the accent, but dude. Dr. Deming begins introducing me to new faces when a man loudly calls someone's name, perhaps *mine*. The second time he's almost barking it and I turn and see a guy from the Duty-Free shop hoisting my extra-large bottle of Quality Citron Vodka into the air while slowly, and *extra-loudly*, enunciating my full name. I'm mortified.

He is not supposed to deliver alcohol until I'm securely seated on the plane. I don't want anything to do with this shit right now. I look at him and mentally blast, "NOT NOW!" The eye contact relieves him of further duties after I verify proof of identity and a receipt, I sign

At Charlotte-Douglas International check-in I was told I could have a second carry-on. Yes thank you. I want to carry more stuff. In the Duty-Free Shop I found a Carolina-blue Lacoste bag and made it mine. When I saw alcohol behind the checkout counter I planned ahead.

But now some law-breaking, slack-ass concierge has waltzed up and raised my liquid crutch in front of the whole world. Clearly this guy did NOT read the memo on the rules regarding International rules of alcohol purchase and delivery. He's getting impatient and so he calls out my whole name, "Leslie Suzanne Link." while waving the bottle in the air.

I'm busted so I tell the group, "Excuse me for a second please." I wave my hand high over my head towards the guys and concede, "I'm over here dude." He walks over and has me sign for the ill-timed delivery. I turn back to the group watching the transaction and announce, "Well so much for first impressions. It's nice to meet y'all too!"

*Thank goodness* they all laugh.

Dr. Deming laughs too and inquires, "So you like,"—he looks down at the bag—"*a lot,* of vodka?"

I cringe and blurt out Tourette's style, "I have a *huge* fear of flying. I mean a **seriously huge** fear of flying." Well it is what it is so I elevate the bottle as if it were a trophy and confess, "Look, I know I can't stay drunk for two whole days of flying, but y'all will *never* call me a quitter!"

As they crack up I'm extra thankful that Dr. Deming appears to have a good sense of humor too—or at least a similar one.

Kelly, a 53-year-old fellow cancer survivor welcomes me and asks where I'm sitting. It's at that point I realize we're not all sitting together, and that I may be drinking alone. I report, "Some people say, 'Drinking doubles alone don't make it a party.' I say they need better attitudes."

I know she's heard that old country song by Barbara Mandrel when she laughs and nods her head enthusiastically. "Don't worry, you won't be drinking alone." She's only two rows right behind me.

At 7:10 p.m., we board a KLM Royal Dutch airlines flight to Amsterdam. It's the biggest plane I've ever been on and I'm positive if it crashes, it'll leave a mark.

When I get to my seat I notice the person seated on my right is wearing an A+BC shirt. At 72, he's the oldest in our group and introduces himself as Frank from Iowa, a fellow cancer survivor. His niece is on board and that makes him Uncle Frank.

I tell him, "Oh that's wonderful to have family with you. Can you be my Uncle Frank too?" He readily accepts my invitation to become instant family.

Kelly calls out my name and I raise my hands in thumbs up. I know what she wants and I like her already. I try to get to the vodka, but it's wrapped in plastic, surrounded by cardboard, and stapled together. I explain to Uncle Frank about my deep fear of flying while I deconstruct the wrapping. I get to the bottle but the silver cap is sealed in plastic with no perforations. I'm getting impatient so I start to use my teeth. Uncle Frank sticks his hand in front of my mouth and intercepts the bottle.

"Thanks, Uncle Frank. Your next drunk is on me." I raise the cup for emphasis.

He chuckles and shakes his head, "That's not necessary."

I promise him, "No, dude, *really, I* got your back."

Someone behind us asks Uncle Frank a question as he returns the open bottle to me. I hand him my cup of ice to hold so I can fill it easier and hear the voice from the rear say, "Thank you, Father Frank."

Wait, what?! *Father* Frank? I make purposeful eye contact, "*Please,* Uncle Frank. Tell me you have a *tangible* son sitting behind us?"

He laughs and tilts my cup toward me for easier pouring. It turns out he's a Catholic priest *and* a most gracious wingman.

As we taxi down the runway he asks if I'd like him to say a prayer. *Indeed* I do want him to do that. I grab his hand with both of mine and he rests his free one on top of the pile. He prays aloud a beautiful and soothing prayer. I cry when he asks God, "Please keep Your cheek especially close to Suzanne's, and bring her peace." He squeezes my hand as I end his prayer with, "And thank you God for Uncle Frank's seat assignment. Amen."

Shortly after the fasten seatbelt sign is turned off Kelly appears at the end of my row, smiling and requesting vodka. She leans over a couple of strangers to whisper, "But Dr. Deming says we need to be *discreet.*"

Holy cow, he feels the need to state a no-brainer. Have I already stained the relationship with my first impression? I can't worry about that because if I don't calm my anxiety and I end up freaking out at over 35,000 ft., I could stain a lot worse.

After about four hours, we're halfway to Amsterdam. Among other things I've nailed the USA Today crossword and puzzles, and posted a personal best on the ones in the *New York Times* as well. As I ponder why I ever let my fear of flying get so out of control, a flight attendant's voice pierces through the intercom, "Will any medical doctors on board please come to the front left side of the plane?" We have four in our group and they stand in unison.

One of ours, Dr. Charlie, specializes in Internal Medicine in Iowa. He figures out what happened and after consulting with the pilots, the decision is made to continue to Amsterdam. There an ambulance will be waiting to transport the patient to Amsterdam University Hospital.

I turn around in my seat and crouch on my knees. When I get Kelly's attention I hold my hand out and whisper over a few rows, "Please pass the bottle back, *discreetly*." I've only had two drinks, so this third one's gonna need to be stiff.

We're half way across the Atlantic and a man just had a life-threatening stroke. This has to be the worst place ever to have a medical emergency.

I'll soon find out I'm wrong; this is nowhere near the worst place.

Departing the Queen City

With Brad at airport

# 5

# AK-47s and a Holding Cell

We arrive at Schiphol International Airport in Amsterdam on Sunday at 9:05 a.m. local time. Guards sporting AK-47s carry out security. By sporting, I mean carrying the weapon in a constant ready-to-use manner. The guards are all fit, focused, and *fine*. They wear bluish-gray camouflage uniforms and red berets that look like the cherry on top of *badass*. I've never been in a public place with this level of military presence and, dare I say, *hotness*.

    As Kelly and I walk we discuss the armed officers and agree, the sheer number of men, and therefore AK-47s, seems excessive, and *unnerving*. After more walking, I tell Kelly I want to give her the vodka because it's heavy and I won't be drinking anymore of it.

    When I'd started to leave it on the plane she'd said I should take it in case someone in the group wanted a drink later. I did but now I have a bad feeling. I'm terrible at deciphering accents and wish I'd paid closer attention to the flight attendant with the thick Dutch one. She said a lot of stuff at once to me as I gathered my belongings to deplane. What if she'd told me to leave the vodka?

Kelly hesitates then declines. She's not comfortable carrying *potential contraband* either. We agree I'll dump it, but disposal will be in front of gun-wielding guards with cameras at every turn. Forget that Schiphol International is Europe's busiest airport. As an ignorant tourist, I fear the worst – like getting shot or locked up like on the TV show called *Locked Up Abroad*. The series highlights tourists with prison sentences in foreign countries in shocking conditions.

My fear increases to paranoia, which leads to defensiveness, and then to the thought, "Screw the Dutch. How bad can an Amsterdam jail really be? They probably sit around smoking weed, reading pointers on how to plant tulips, and whittling wooden shoes."

I'm not sure, but this may *not* be sound reasoning and I want to ditch this bottle stat. I know I have to leave it somewhere without cameras or guards, which means a bathroom. The closest Ladies restroom has a line out the door, as do the second and third ones.

When I get close to my gate I see fellow A+BCers gathering to go through another security check. It's now or never so I go to the closest restroom and wait. There are only three tiny stalls and I get the one in the middle. I hang my blue bag with the vodka in it on the door's hook and take the bottle out to leave on the floor. But I realize it can easily be seen by the person on either side of me and I can't chance running into the one random stranger that's always wanted to be a cop or some hero that could take this thing south.

I pretend to flush and cover the bottle with my blue bag, hugging them both against my chest. The bag's handles flap in my face and beg the question, "Why aren't you using us?"

Instead of a door, the restroom is recessed behind a short wall that doesn't even come to the floor. As I stand at the entrance/exit and watch three *uber-armed* security soldiers, I'm struck again by the complete lack of privacy afforded in this airport.

Earlier I didn't want the vodka to become my legacy in this *group*. Now I pray the alcohol won't end up my legacy in this *country*.

The top of the bottle has already come off twice, spilling vodka on the floor of the plane, and then in my bag, so the wrapping is warped. For a split-second the line is empty so I smush the vodka into the corner of the short exit wall. The bottle falls over yet again, but this time onto cement. The glass clinks loudly and I wait just long enough to see if liquid will stream unchecked, under the wall onto the concourse. It hasn't *yet,* so I haul ass. I don't dare slow down until I'm at the gate, camouflaged by red tee shirts.

Our group is already going through the next security checkpoint so I don't have to evade trigger happy Rambos' much longer. Wait, what? How did I get from being embarrassed by signing for a bottle of vodka in Detroit, to fearing being gunned down for that same bottle in Amsterdam?

How many hours has it been since I left Charlotte? If this level of unraveling is exponential, I'll be in a straight-jacket by the time we land in Nepal. I'm sure I'm exaggerating but seriously, I'd love a "Thunder Shirt."

Kelly calls to me from the side of the line cleared to travel to India, "Where've you been? What took you so long?" I shake my head and motion her forward. I'll explain later how possibly, thanks to her, I narrowly escaped a Holland prison.

I collapse into a chair at the departure gate, so relieved to be free of alcohol. Now I only have two more hours to think about the next very long plane ride. As time seems to crawl, I get more and more nervous until I'm taunted by a single thought, "I wish I had alcohol."

At 11:15 a.m., we board the eight hour flight to India. After a short period, dinner is served, and soon after that, the cabin lights go off. It takes a while, but when I finally get comfortable enough to drift off, the overhead lights come back on and breakfast service begins. This can't be right. I open the window shade for proof that I'm wrong, and indeed, I see the sun rising on the horizon.

Night and day are shifting on fast-forward and the effect is disorienting. I've never thought about time changes, much less their relations to the earth's rotation, because I've never traveled so far in one direction. However, on this trip, I've flown through multiple time zones into a brand new day, without the normal passage of time.

The body's internal 24-hour clock mirrors the sun's 24-hour cycle; it contracts or expands to remain in synchronicity. Traveling east is the hardest because the day is shortened and the body has to cut its natural cycle even further.

When we land in New Delhi at 10:50 p.m. local time, we're escorted into a large holding area to be processed by immigration. Bikal, a Program Director for A+BC and a Nepali native, warns us that we'll be here for a while. He explains the airport still uses carbon paper, hand-written tickets, and manually posted information. Wait a tic, don't a lot of US tech companies use India-based companies in their call centers? I've been told it's not uncommon for baggage handlers here to be highly educated with graduate degrees. These people are fully aware of computers and technology, so I don't get it.

Several groups are huddled tightly as if in meetings. Some of them must have been here a long time; they're clearly getting impatient. Groups send representatives to the counter and some of them raise their voices at airport employees. *Is this our future?*

We've gathered in one section and I find myself sitting next to our videographer/photographer John Richard. I notice one of his cameras is the same as the one I got a few years ago for Christmas, a Canon 7D. It's very advanced and complicated for my skill level, but I've read a brief synopsis about it so I offer to help, "Hey John, I have that same camera so if you need an assistant let me know."

His look is full of surprise, amusement, and appreciation. I somehow get that owning a pocket knife doesn't make me surgical assistant. What I a doofus. Another outstanding first impression.

Dr. Deming suggests we practice Qigong, a Chinese holistic system of coordinated body posture and movement, breathing, and meditation.

Judith steps forward to lead us and as soon as I lay eyes on her, my breathing slows. She's a 59-year-old cancer survivor that comes across as a peaceful Angel. She's petite with short graying hair and round Waldo glasses that give her an air of fun and good humor.

I'm glad to participate, but I'm self-conscious trying to exhibit balance and flexibility. I can't walk a straight line, much less balance on one leg while elevating and contorting the other one. I scan the group to find someone with similar balance challenges, but everyone else seems smooth. As I wonder if I'm the most awkward person here, I hear laughter behind me and see the handsome couple John and his wife Mary from Minnesota (I'll make the distinction between the Johns by including our videographer's last name – John *Richard*). Mary says she and John are uncoordinated so I recognize them as *my* people, and take a step back to join them.

In their mid-forties with three children, they're here as caregivers. Mary works for the American Cancer Society and has dark pixie-styled hair, gorgeous eyes with eyelashes galore, and a striking shade of red lipstick. John is tall and handsome with hazel eyes. He's an accountant for a big company and true to stereotypes, he's more low-key.

I instantly feel comfortable with them and after the exercises, Mary and I lay on the floor, feet propped on chairs, working our respective crossword puzzles. John's nearby but it strikes me that while they're a close and loving couple, they're also independent people, each on their own journey.

After several more hours in the holding area, we're *finally* processed through International Transfers and able to move into the main part of the airport. The Indira Gandhi International airport is South Asia's largest, with a capacity to handle over 30 million passengers a year. But after eight and a half hours in this place, I'm not impressed.

# 6

# The Other Side of the World

At 7:30 a.m. we board our final flight to Nepal's Tribhuvan International Airport. An hour and a half later, we land in Kathmandu. After two full days of travel to the other side of the world, *I'm knuckle-draggin' tired.*

When I step outside the airport, I see a city that doesn't make sense. It's old and brown, and somehow crooked. This amazing place expands further than I can see, and though it lays so low, it never seems to disappear.

On the ride to the hotel, Nepali native Bikal gives us first-hand information. A few years after assisting Charlie Wittmack on a summit of Mt. Everest, he was able to move his family to the United States. He chose Iowa as his home state, and became an integral part of A+BC.

He explains how scaffolding is used during construction and is made of bamboo because it's widely available and economic. The plant's stem is stronger than wood, brick, or concrete, and it has a tensile strength that rivals steel. But because many stems have to be joined vertically for height, the buildings soon appear to sway. Now the off-kilter appearance and absence of skyscrapers makes sense.

In stark contrast, the Queen City Charlotte, NC, is a major banking center, obsessed with her own image. Sky scrapers race each other upward in competition to stand the tallest and grandest. They dress in glass and steel to create mirrors, into which they reflect on their success. Each towering structure is perfected with adorning water fountains, sculptures, and immaculate landscaping.

By contrast, the buildings in Kathmandu are haggard and slumping. Landscaping is irrelevant. There's a complete absence of structure, direction, and organization creates acceptable functioning chaos. There are no stoplights, stop signs, street signs, lanes, or curbs; electrical wires are hung on crooked poles that intersect haphazardly in random places, often hanging low in the center of intersections.

There are no sidewalks. Storefronts often sit across trenches through which the city's filth flows, and pedestrians walk. Most people wear a mask as protection from whatever is set airborne by this living city. I sense there's more men than women, more young than old, and a lot of people wear school uniforms. I'm shocked by the number of unattended children.

The streets are dotted with the occasional cow, sacred and not to be eaten. With the right of way and nothing better to do, the bovine animals roam the streets eating garbage and flicking flies.

Our bus winds its way through the dirt streets flooded with people, mopeds, cars, buses, and cavernous potholes. But here's the kicker—accidents seem to be rare and usually not serious…again, impossible to comprehend. I'm witnessing organized chaos.

There are obviously serious problems in this third world government, and the whole city screams, "**Safety Hazard!**"

We check into our five-star hotel which seems at odds with most of the city. It's large and grand and as we gather in the atrium we're greeted with cold juice that tastes like *Tang*. I'm certain of one truth in this moment – if Heaven has a flavor, it's *Tang*.

At this time we're given our room and roommate assignments. The name called with mine is Ruth, a 62- year-old sarcoma survivor from Minnesota. She's pretty, slender, blue-eyed with curly blonde hair. She lost her dominant left arm to cancer nine years ago and she's become miraculously ambidextrous. She's worked with therapists and personal trainers to become 100% self-sufficient, and she trained for this trip Ninja style. She has core strength, stamina, and balance to rival that of a Cirque de Sole performer. I'm not even in her *shadow's* league.

At 6:30 p.m. we gather in the lobby to go to dinner. I can see Dr. Deming meeting with a Nepali couple in a room off the lobby. The handsome man is our head Sherpa, Lhakpa. He's fit, Nepali tan, with dark hair, a striking jaw, and a quiet air of strength and wisdom. I notice his wife, Ang Lhakpa, who is wrapping a long white prayer scarf called a *khatak* around Dr. Deming's neck. She hugs him with purpose and it's obvious, this isn't their first meeting.

I'm told they first met Dr. Deming in April 2011 when both Ang Lhakpa and Lhakpa were Sherpa on A+BC's trip to Everest's base camp. Eight weeks later, Dr. Deming received a call from Lhakpa, telling him Ang Lhakpa had leukemia. Dr. Deming was able to work with a pharmaceutical company to get her treatment and medications, and other sources made it possible for her to take a monthly flight to Kathmandu from her home in

Khumjung, for lab work. It's understandable why they both adore Dr. Deming so much.

By the time we head out to dinner it's already dark. To get to the restaurant, we wind through back alleyways and heavily congested streets.

I remember my last conversation with my best friend Martha, it was on the way to the airport two days ago. She called to say good-bye for yet another final time, but on this last call she emphasized, "*Never ever* go out at night alone in Kathmandu, *for any reason.*"

My reply was tinted with sarcasm, "Why would I go out at night alone?"

She chided me, "I know you *wouldn't*, but promise me you *won't*. Do you hear me? I mean it, *Suzanne.*"

Her voice came through the car's speakers clearly, and I flinched when she called me by my name. Normally she'd jibber jabber whatever configuration of words that popped-up in her head – but she was making a point now.

"O.K., we *all* hear you, and I promise, Martha, I won't go out at night alone." I turned to Emma in the back seat and gave an eye roll.

Emma checked me loudly, "You better listen and do what she says Mama."

Martha asks, "Emma, did she just roll her eyes? Tell your mother, *I'm very serious.*"

My next look at Emma shot the question, "Why'd you give me up?"

I turned back to face Martha's chastisement head-on, "I know you're serious and *I swear,* I won't go out at night alone."

I turned back to Emma, only to be blasted, "You can get mad all you want Mama, but you don't know everything, and this is a big deal." Then with a touch of inherited sarcasm she stung, "But you read a pamphlet one time."

I shot back with my own air of certainty, "You don't know everything either. Martha keeps me up to date."

Emma laughed so suddenly and loudly I flinched, "Why? What's so funny?"

She could barely contain herself, "I'm sure she does Mama. You'll be fine."

"*'But still'* what? What's Martha *not* telling me?"

"I don't know everything Martha *has* and *hasn't* told you, but she's ..." Brad cuts Emma off and changes the subject.

Being in Kathmandu I now understand that getting lost in the daylight would be easy enough, but in the dark, it's *probable.* When crossing the busier streets, we hold hands and Ruth extends her left arm with instructions, "Grab Stumper, he won't fall off!"

Justin, a 28-year-old brain cancer survivor from Iowa, and Staff member with A+BC, leads the way. One of Dr. Deming's blog posts sums Justin perfectly, "He's our team musician and, in some ways, our team puppy dog. His fun-loving, easy-going attitude and his Hollywood smile hide the fact that he lives with an underlying anxiety; his brain tumor may recur someday."

Justin's so cool his guitar gets its own Sherpa.

The restaurant Fire & Ice is packed with a lobby that reminds me of Vail Colorado, but with trekkers instead of skiers. These are young, fit, good-looking guys, seeking athletic adventure. My god, I feel so old.

Sitting across from me is Teresa, a volunteer staff member for A+BC. She's in her mid-fifties with shoulder length blonde hair and glasses, but she could easily pass for 20 years younger. She's fit and healthy by design and effort, engaging in regular workouts, yoga, and cycling. I'm about to fall out of my chair from fatigue, but she's still full stride.

As about 40 of us try to group order pizza, the discussion devolves into the differences between pizzas in the US, then more specifically, in Iowa. Teresa's role with A+BC is "the Git 'er done Girl," and that's exactly what she does. She orders a variety of pizzas and when more are needed, she gets them too. She seems decisive and efficient and her laugh is a contagious mixture of howl, stop, gasp, higher pitched hoot-to-howl.

After what turns out to be the best pizza on the *planet*, we head back into the maze. I know we're retracing our steps, but nothing feels very familiar. Retail ebbs and flows, often blurring together. The shops are mostly on the ground level, and apartments fill the modest few levels above. Every window sill, tiny balcony, and rooftop, is alive with people. Some are cooking, some are doing laundry, and some are simply observing.

So many people live here, it makes all the air feel *occupied*.

By the time we get back to the hotel I've decided two things: 1) Martha has no worries, I would *never under any circumstances* go out at night alone. And 2) Kathmandu has to be the easiest place on earth to get lost, so only an idiot or a fool would *ever* let that happen.

Kathmandu, Nepal

Bamboo Scaffolding

# 7

# Everything Old Is New Again

It's 3:30 a.m. Why can't I sleep? I'm not hungry, I'm not hot or cold. My hypervigilance isn't new. I learned at an early age to be extra alert at night. Sleep and I became estranged when I was around five and by the time I was twenty, we were divorced.

While parts of my childhood were ideal, parts were traumatizing. My *almost high-enough* functioning alcoholic father, Don, was stereotypical in many ways; unreliable and unpredictable, sometimes a happy drunk, and occasionally violent with my mother. When I became my Mom's self-appointed protector, I grew up on fast-forward.

By the time I was seven, I was a veteran in dealing with my volatile alcoholic father. Don's two favorite places in Tuscaloosa were the liquor store, and Jackie's Lounge, which closed at two a.m. I had to stay awake to protect my mother in the event the Don came home violent. Fortunately that wasn't often, but when he did, it was terrifying. The lack of predictability and control created chronic hypervigilance, much of which is still present.

To stay awake, I kept a bowl of water by my bed, and I'd splash on my eyes constantly. My defense weapon of choice was my metal baton. With the rubber tips removed, it was no longer a toy to twirl, but rather a steel rod to serve as a wake to find the baton lying beside me and I'd grab it hard, shake it, and blame it for letting me fall asleep.

It was a silly thought and a silly weapon, but I counted on it to save my Mom. Luckily, Don's violence was seldom, but it was also random and variable. His behavior was completely unpredictable, so I had to stay on high alert, and especially on the weekends.

Around 2:30 in the morning I'd hear his two-toned green Ford truck rounding the curve in front of Mu and Turtle's house. That was my cue to get up and meet him at the door with the same performance; an alert and happy child. I'd make small talk in the kitchen while he fried bologna for sandwiches, splattering grease everywhere, and leaving the kitchen a shit hole for my Mom to clean.

Chances were good she'd hand him his ass on a platter the next morning, but by then, he'd be sober, and she'd have temporarily forgotten she's a Christian.

After tucking the drunk in on the couch, I'd lay and listen for him to start snoring. Finally, in thee wee hours of the morning, I could sleep.

I was beyond grateful when my parents finally divorced after 18 years of marriage, but by the age of 12, the emotional damage had left scars.

My high need for control came to me honestly. *Thank goodness for therapy.*

By the age of 12, my nerves had created stomach problems. I'd try to be quiet when throwing up, so I wouldn't wake my Mom. If I woke her, she'd be irritated. She didn't fear Don and thought I was being too sensitive, in fact downright silly. She had the coping skills of an adult, and she needed me to be a little soldier. I wasn't soldier material, yet, but I complied with all my might.

My insecurities came to me honestly. *Thank goodness for therapy.*

I was diagnosed with a duodenal ulcer at 19 and by the time I was 23, I experienced generalized anxiety and occasional night terrors. At my mother's encouragement I went to see a psychologist, even though I thought therapy was for weak people; I made sure to tell the psychologist so.

When she asked about my childhood, I informed her that anyone that used their childhood as an excuse, was the weakest of the weak. She didn't push me on it, but she requested I attend a support group meeting for Adult Children of Alcoholics (ACA). When I snorted and rolled my eyes she made it a challenge; damn it, now I *had* to go.

I found a meeting nearby and arriving late, I took a seat close to the door. "Participation Optional" was stated, so I planned to bide my time until I'd kept my word, and then I'd haul ass. A list of the "Common Characteristics of Adult Children of Alcoholics" was passed around and those who chose to participate read one aloud. My attention was immediately engaged because I was relating *big time.*

1. "I judge myself without mercy."
2. "I take myself very seriously."
3. "I feel different from other people."

The list was mind-numbingly accurate.

4. "I have difficulty with intimate relationships."

By the time the list got to me, I couldn't wait to read aloud, "I overreact to changes over which I have no control."

I swallowed hard and passed the paper. I wanted to *bawl!*

5. "I constantly seek approval and affirmation."

Could it be true? I'm not a defective loser-freak, and in fact, I have a *label!* It would be five years until I'd become a Licensed Professional Counselor (LPC), but the beginning of my therapeutic journey started that night, with that group. I pursued information like it was the Holy Grail, and made self-awareness my number one goal. Stephen Hawking said, "Life would be tragic if it weren't funny." I agree, so my life may be a "Comedy of Errors," but it'll never be a "Greek Tragedy."

Through my own therapeutic process I identified the most extreme parts of myself, and for efficiency, I named them. Alice is one extreme part and yes, as in Wonderland. She's the part of me who blindly loves and trusts, and gets crushed easily. She sees the world as magnificent, and has grand ideas and dreams. In her sensitivity, she loves and hurts in equally deep amounts. Alice shrinks in fear, anxiety, and insecurity, always certain she's *not good enough.*

The other extreme part of me exists to protect Alice, which means countering fear and energy with equal intensity. This part of me has a take-no-prisoner's attitude and I call her as Janis, as in Janis Joplin. Full of pain and self-doubt, Joplin had a gut wrenching need for affirmation from others. Although she was the greatest female Rock Star in the *world*, existential depression and insecurities gnawed at her soul. To cover her pain and vulnerability, she adopted a tough as nails personae that both pushed and pulled at people.

My own personal Janis can be fierce. She asks for forgiveness rather than permission, and she doesn't care what other people think. She's impatient with those that aren't in fifth gear, but she'll fight tirelessly for an underdog. She is 100% going to protect Alice at all cost, so if in the meantime someone's feelings get hurt, well that's just tough shit.

As my healthiest self, I travel life as a balanced and rational adult except when I should **HALT**. I subscribe to the acronym HALT – never get too **H**ungry, too **A**ngry, too **L**onely, or too **T**ired. Those states of being can't support your best self.

On this journey, I experience *otherworldly* levels of HALT and get way too hungry, too angry, too lonely, and too tired.

As a result, Janis and Alice make appearances and curtain calls.

*Thank goodness for therapy.*

# 8

# Dream Girl

I quit pretending to sleep at 4:30, so at 4:50 I'm the first to breakfast. The dining room is empty and the staff is still setting up the breakfast buffet. A waiter sets a hot bin of scrambled eggs between the trays of bread and baked beans. The beans look like they were poured right out of a can of Van Camps pork and beans which I like, but I'm not *bean-for-breakfast hungry.* I decide to stick with the recognizable meats, but mostly with the cheese, and fruit.

At the end of the buffet table, I see glorious pitchers of orange and yellow liquids. This hydration has to be safe; it's in a pitcher. The moment it became unsafe to drink the water I got terribly thirsty, and now I can't get enough liquids. I hope so hard the orange pitcher has Heaven's Tang.

The glasses are tiny, so I carry as many as I can at once. I make several trips until I think I've collected the maximum before drawing attention. It's still just the staff and me, so I'm almost comfortable being so awkward.

I'm not hungry but food is fuel, so I eat eggs, cheese, potatoes, and a roll. When I ask the waiter how much I owe for breakfast, he shrugs. Maybe that's body language for something specific. The meal may be included with the room, but I'm not risking a "dine and dash charge." I leave enough money by my plate to pay for a "Waffle House All American Breakfast" with a generous tip, and then double that amount to make sure.

No one in our group has come to breakfast yet, so I walk out into the courtyard. It's still dark but I can make out a familiar silhouette. It belongs to Dr. Charlie. His neck is so stiff he can't turn his head enough to see who's coming, so his torso leads the way.

I feel his pain and do some gut-praying that I don't get any neck, shoulder, or lower back problems on this trip. I was told eight years ago I'd need back surgery within a year. I went to a chiropractor and neuromuscular massage therapist for a few years after that, and so far I've beaten the odds. But I'm very aware this trekking stuff will bring challenges.

Dr. Charlie's so tight he's walking like a crab—his left side arrives before the right one. After two days of airplane travel, he's out of alignment, with one shoulder higher than the other and his hips askew. I know he's in pain.

After we commiserate over common maladies, I press my elbow into the right crook of his neck and shoulder until eventually, the knotted muscles begin loosening. I apply a little more pressure and the knots shrink more, but he whines. The next round of elbow pressure and the sound he makes is mournful and pitiful. I think with my mouth and hope I don't offend, "Dude, really? If you don't have a plan B, you're gonna need to toughen up *significantly*. I'm not sure, but I don't think it gets easier from here."

His laughter is loud and hearty before the sun even gets out of pajamas! I'm making a new friend.

After breakfast everyone gathers in the yard and Judith leads us in what will become a daily ritual of Qigong. For the morning meditation Dr. Deming reads from John O'Donohue's book, *To Bless the Space between Us*. Today's poem is about compassion—"sympathetic consciousness of others' distress together with a desire to alleviate it." When he closes the book, he tells us, "It will get difficult at different times, for different people, for different reasons. We'll all be tested. What I hope will emerge from each of us is *compassion*."

I scan the group to see who might need my compassion sooner rather than later. Every single person looks a million times better than I feel, so I go back to minding my own business.

I've noticed several new faces that Dr. Deming introduces as the west coast arrivals. It's the mother and daughter duo that stand out to me the most. Kristin, 22, is a leukemia survivor and her mother Leslie, 51, is here as a caregiver. They are both beautiful and petite, with gorgeous smiles. From a distance, the biggest difference I can see is that Leslie has blonde hair and blue eyes while Kristin has black hair and brown eyes. I can't imagine how hard it would be to have your child have cancer and I hope it's not wrong to pray I never know.

I suddenly miss Emma so much. I wish she could magically appear beside me for this journey. I know she can't, so I sure hope these two are good people. I feel an urge to connect with them.

When we get on the bus, I experience this living and breathing city all over again. People, vehicles and random animals create sluggish traffic. I'm on the left side by a window while we creep through traffic. The bus is almost at a crawl when I notice her.

My eye is drawn by the sunlight on her long, silky, dark hair. It falls all the way down her back and I think, "It's so dusty and dirty out there, she needs a shower cap. Do they have shower caps here?"

She's a young female and I wonder why she's alone, how old she is, and where she's going. She isn't wearing a uniform but has a full backpack that looks heavy. I hope she doesn't have far to go and wonder how far she's come. She's walking and I'm riding. We're both surrounded by people, places, and things, yet our eyes meet and neither of us looks away.

I feel my right hand rising. Both of her hands are rising too. I wave slowly and mouth "hello" as she pulls her mask down. She mouths Namaste as she brings her hands together in front of her face. We both smile widely, eyes crinkled, then she covers her mouth with her hand. The gesture feels familiar; my heart knows hers and mine swells, as do the tears in my eyes.

I'm aware this is the girl from my dream, the girl from the Vaudevillian Theatre. She's a bit older, but I'd know her anywhere. I want to tell her so, but the bus takes a sharp right turn and she's gone, out of my view, out of my life. My knee-jerk reaction is to stand up and yell, "Stop the bus, I gotta get off!" But then what? Exchange friendship bracelets?

Besides, I think that's what we just did.

The Hotel Malla, Kathmandu, Nepal

Ruth and Dr. Deming take time to journal at the hotel

# 9

## A Living Doll

Our first stop is a palace in the center of the city at the home of a real living goddess. She's the Kumari, the manifestation of divine female energy. She's from a Buddhist family—but she's a Hindu goddess.

She must be without blemish. To avoid confusion, the senior Buddhist priests who select the Kumari have created a list of "thirty-two perfections of a goddess including: neck like a conch shell; body like a banyan tree; eyelashes like a cow; thighs like a deer; chest like a lion; voice soft and clear as a duck's. In addition, her hair and eyes should be very black, she should have dainty hands and feet, and small and well-recessed sexual organs."

If you were to be literal about these perfections, she'd look like Gollum from The Lord of the Rings.

Once the candidate is chosen, she undergoes rigorous tests, one of which is "black night" in which 108 goats and buffaloes are beheaded and sacrificed to the goddess Kali. The severed heads are spread in the temple courtyard, illuminated with candles, and danced around by masked men. The candidate has to spend the night alone with the animal heads and if she shows fear, another candidate begins the process.

I can't escape my identity as a psychotherapist and I'm obsessing over this child's lack of an *appropriate developmental curve*—from child, to goddess, to spectacle, *overnight*. She leaves the premises for festivals and public appearances only, and she's carried everywhere within and without these palace walls.

Her palace is a three-storied brick building decorated with intricate woodcarvings. We enter the courtyard and I notice the second story is skirted by a balcony. As I wait to see a child goddess, I sense *Alice levels* of compassion, sadness, and curiosity. I feel the urge to cry but Janis intervenes, "Holy shit, this is straight out of the dream!"

I look around the courtyard and maintain denial, "No, it's not."

"Ha ha, *yes*, it is. It's *exactly* like it. You're in a space surrounded by a balcony, but instead of velvet curtains, the walls are wooden. And you're here in a group of people waiting to see a child appear, aha ha ha ha, on *a balcony!*"

The parallels are striking and I don't feel like crying anymore. I'm highly aware of the similarities between this place and my dream. I'm getting highly uncomfortable, but when the Kumari walks onto the balcony, I get mesmerized.

She's stunning and sad, beautiful and tragic, majestic, and somehow, hollow. She *is* the little girl from my dream. I stand up taller to minimize the distance between us.

I'm using my best Jedi mind-control to will the Kumari to eye contact, but she doesn't look down. I look at the people around me, all looking at this girl, and I just want her to look down and into *any* of our faces.

I want her to know, "I see *you*. You're a goddess to the people in Nepal, but to *me*, you're a little girl in paint and costume. You've had to forfeit your childhood for religious views and ceremonies you're way too young to understand, let alone for which to give, "Informed Consent."

I consider myself to be open-minded to other belief systems, but this situation screams child abuse to me.

I was raised Southern Baptist with a lot of "do's" and "don'ts." I challenged them later in life, but as a kid, I was ruled by fear. Guilt, shame, and fear were the emotional staples of the Sunday sermons as delivered by Brother Stillman. He was one of the most committed and passionate people I'd ever met, (he always will be, may he RIP). He was 5'3," barrel-shaped, and joyous, except when preaching. That was all about saving souls, and he'd get seriously riled up.

The goal was to save souls from a literal burning hell of fire, eternal damnation, teeth gnashing, and crawling worms. Hell sounded terrifying except for the worms. The worms just weren't that scary, in comparison.

The "Invitation" at sermon's end was a call to leave the pew, kneel at the altar around the pulpit, and repent of your sins. Empty pews meant we were sorry and with so many vacated, you couldn't help but notice those unrepentant souls still in the pews singing. They were probably hell bound if Jesus came back in the clouds sooner than later.

Getting saved meant saying "The Sinner's Prayer," asking to be forgiven of your sins, and accepting Jesus Christ as your

Lord and Savior. Your name gets written in the Lamb's Book of Life so when you die, Saint Peter checks you in at pearly gates. If your name isn't in the book, then it's straight to hell for you. I wondered if Saint Peter ever got tired of saying, "Go to hell."

Terrifying thoughts plagued me as a child. What if I said the prayer wrong? What if the admin angel didn't spell my name right? The Southern Baptist religion is unforgiving so I always wanted to get "it" right.

I tried for a long time to subscribe to the religious prescriptions of my youth, but the margins of tolerance for right and wrong proved too narrow, rigid, and unforgiving. In many ways, the Southern Baptist religion was psychologically harmful to me, but because it was touted as the absolute truth by my elders, I didn't question it until my mid-teens.

As I stand here looking up at this child goddess, I wonder who's to say who's right or wrong. I make another note to myself, "Don't judge what you don't understand."

The goddess turns to look over the rail to her left, so I turn my gaze to see what's worth her attention. There's a man squatting over a fire and making bread in a pan. As I watch him, it occurs to me that observing the process of any creation must be infinitely more interesting than looking into the faces of countless tourists, for which she's *an attraction*.

What must she think of us? I want her to know we're different from other tourists, but I have no way of knowing that for sure. Maybe if you've seen one tourist from a balcony as a child goddess, you've seen them all. We're probably the fish in her bowl.

Alice explodes with love for this little girl and wants to yell, "I love you so much!" Instead, I bury my face in a tissue. I don't dare exhale. When I look up again she's still watching the man making bread and I wonder if she's hungry. That bread smells fabulous.

On the bus, I can't stop thinking about the goddess and wonder out loud, "How long is a term? When does a new Kumari take over?"

Bikal is sitting nearby and answers, "When the current one becomes a woman."

Oh, I see … around twelve or thirteen? "Then what does she do?"

He thinks for a second, "She retires."

While I sure wouldn't want her gig, there is something to be said for early retirement.

The Kumari's Palace

A recent Kumari (Stock Photo)

# 10

## Is This Bob Seger's Kathmandu?

We continue to explore this complex of beautiful temples and shrines, both Hindu and Buddhist. Most were built in the Pagoda Style between the 12$^{th}$ and 18$^{th}$ centuries and embellished with intricately wood-carved accents.

  Durbar Square epitomizes the religious and cultural life of the Nepali people. Kings are still crowned here and their coronations played out among these ancient structures. Along the palaces are quadrangle-shaped courtyards and ancient temples. The heart of the Square is bustling with vendors selling necklaces, wide silver bracelets, silk purses, wooden flutes, lacquered bowls, and a plethora of statues and masks. Some are locally made but much is imported from their northern neighbor, China.

  When our tour guide stops to point out something, the vendors stop with us. I've made several purchases so by the time we get to the other end of the Square, I'm feeling encased in vendors. Every view I have is framed with goods for sale. The same people are always up front and it doesn't take long to figure out the strict pecking order in Nepal: male over female and old over young.

The men shout at the women to "back off" which they do. I know their cultural norms are different from ours and I want to be respectful, but injustice triggers me. I bite my tongue and look directly at the females when I'm interested in something they have. I think about how little control young females have here. Do they feel powerless or is it simply their norm?

One male in particular seems to be the leader and barks orders. He's been trying to sell me a small silver Tibetan Prayer Wheel with the top adorned in turquoise and coral stones. When you take the top off, it reveals a handwritten scroll on charred parchment paper. It's beautiful, but costs more than everything I've bought so far. I can't get comfortable with the price, so I decline.

He's persistent, but never invasive. A couple times, he yells for the crowd to step back and give me more space; for which I'm grateful. But I don't feel unsafe. There's nothing sneaky or manipulative about these people. They're simply trying to make a living.

Our group joins the rest of A+BC sitting on the steps of the Maju Deval temple, often referred to as the Hippy Temple. Bob Seger's song "Katmandu" made the temple famous in the 1970's and the hippies descended. Approximately 20 men in military camouflage sit on the highest steps. I wonder why they're here and whether it's safe. What's the crime rate and should I know this information? I bet Martha knows and that's why she made a point of telling me not to go out at night alone.

I get the feeling I may *need* the prayer wheel so I look for the guy in charge. Many of the vendors have followed us and now surround the base of the temple. When I find him in the crowd he's about four layers of people deep, but he's looking right at me. I throw out my final offer and he accepts.

I pass money to him via three or four other people and get distracted by a little girl in a blue-green dress. She's on the small side of five and she's followed us from the beginning, typically on the periphery, and usually, looking down.

Where are her parents? Where does she sleep? If this a "Slum Dog Millionaire" thing I'm gonna lose it. My childhood was far from perfect but when I was this child's age I ate fresh vegetable less than thirty minutes old, wore adorable clothes my mother sewed, and while I sometimes went to sleep in fear as a child, I did so in my own bed, in my own bedroom, and oh no, it's *soooo* not fair… on *Holly Hobby **flannel*** sheets. I want to cry.

When someone asks me to see the prayer wheel, I realize I don't have it yet.

I should have known better, so I chalk the money off. But when I look to where I last saw the guy, he's in the same spot, holding the prayer wheel high in the air. He's waiting for me to make eye contact and when I do, he sends the wheel spinning forward. As I watch the safe and expedient progression towards me, my eyes are drawn back to him. He's still watching me. By the time I have it in my hand, I wish I knew the Nepali words for, "I'm sorry I was a doubting asshole."

I mouth, "Thank you" and then shout, "*so much!*" He brings his hands together, mouths Namaste, and bows his head. The literal translation of *Namaste* is "The God in me recognizes and honors the God in you." He just said that very thing to me so I feel guiltier for being a distrusting shit. He raises his head as I bring my hands together and bow my head.

Same note to self, "Stop judging forever and always, period. Shorten this learning curve Suzanne."

As we walk up the steps of another temple, a fellow trekker asks if I'll negotiate with the vendors for her. She wants to buy prayer necklaces, but isn't comfortable; I'm happy to help.

At the top, I start to ask how much the necklaces are when suddenly the vendors start fleeing the temple. I hear someone say that it's illegal to buy and sell in a temple so I grab my friend's hand and start to leave too.

Uniforms advance on us and my instinct tells me to run from anyone wearing blue camouflage. I keep a death grip on my friend and turn to escape in a different direct. Thankfully one of our guides' steps in front of me. He assures us the MP are here for our protection and we're safe. I haven't felt a need to be protected so far, but this *was* kinda scary.

By the time we get back to the bus, I'm being followed by a small army. I look for the little girl in the blue-green dress and spot her at the back of the crowd. I ask no one in particular, but all the while looking at her, "Where's the pretty girl in the blue-green dress?" The crowd opens as I walk toward her. When I kneel in front of her she looks up shyly; I give her my widest smile, "May I see what you have to sell?"

She holds up a rather plain brass bracelet. It's obviously made by hand and has three stones mounted on top. One is blue and the other two are mismatched colors of green. There's a simplicity and humbleness about this bracelet that makes it a piece of artwork to me. I exclaim, "I love this bracelet *so* much! How much is it?" After a pause, she whispers the question, "Five dollars?"

I hand her the all the rupees I empty from the many pockets on my shirt and shorts. It comes close to eight dollars. Then I open my backpack and take out a five-dollar American bill and hand it to her. "And here's the five dollars for the bracelet. Thank you for waiting on me this whole time."

As she takes the money she looks directly into my eyes and beams. There's an adorable space previously occupied by her two front teeth. She bows her head and as her little hands come together, they sandwich the five-dollar bill. Her tiny voice radiates, "Namaste."

I make the same gesture. "And Namaste to you too pretty girl. I really like your dress." I fight back tears because they don't belong here, not now, *not with her.*

I have to board the bus quickly because Alice wants to take this little Angel back to Charlotte, and Janis is already working on the logistics. The little girl in the blue-green dress haunts me, calls to me, and I want to know everything about her. Where's her family and where does she sleep? How many dresses does the little bracelet seller have?"

I warn myself, "Not now. Don't question or feel one more thing; you'll bawl." I ask Bikal about our next stop. He answers, "It's an ancient religious complex, the Swayambhunath Temple. It's also called the Monkey Temple, because there are a lot of monkeys that live there. But do *not* to make eye contact with the monkeys. They take it as a sign of aggression."

I imagine Samurai monkeys wielding banana swords of death, so of course when we arrive, the first thing I do is look at the adorable little monkeys. I wonder where their ninja monkey families hide until it becomes obvious; they don't hide. They're everywhere, doing whatever the hell they want to.

We begin up the hill and one particular monkey seems to be watching me. When I double check, *we make eye-contact.* Oh *ga*-dang it. I don't need this stressor.

The Bagmati River is considered holy by Hindus and Buddhists. Once there we climb a hill with Hindu temples situated along the way, many with painted Shaman meditating on their steps. The river contains large amounts of untreated sewage, as well as garbage from residents in Kathmandu.

Across the river is the Temple of Pashupatinath where the Hindus cremate their dead. The deceased is dipped in the water three times for spiritual purification. I'm not sure what I'm seeing because it doesn't seem real. Each body is wrapped in cloth, laid with marigolds on top, and feet sticking out the bottom. Some of the bodies are being washed while others, further along in the process, have been placed on funeral pyres. Later their ashes will be swept into the river where the "chief mourner" (usually the oldest son) will then bathe. Children are playing in this river, less than ten yards away.

This is insanity to me, but it's just Wednesday to them. I'm still looking over my shoulder for the stalker-monkey.

When we leave the river, we head to Boudhanath Temple, the largest Buddhist Temple outside of Tibet. In the center of the complex is an elevated, giant, gold colored dome, adorned with the Buddha's face. From his head, brightly colored prayer flags sprout to the encircling shops and businesses.

The walkway in between the shops and the Buddha are lined with prayer wheels. Prayer wheels are to be turned clockwise while thinking or speaking the words, "Om mani padme ohm." The mantra is difficult to translate from Sanskrit to English, but its approximation is, "Hail to the jewel in the lotus." This mantra sends the prayer to all corners of the world. Monks are joined by locals as they take their time to stop and spin every prayer wheel, as if drawn by magnetic force.

We eat lunch in a rooftop café overlooking the giant dome. I find myself sitting beside Kristin and I want to adopt her, but Leslie might think differently. Kristin says she likes the prayer bead necklaces I bought in Durbar Square, so I remove the one she points to and wrap it around her wrist. "Here Kristin, take this one please. We'll pray for your luggage with it." Her luggage didn't arrive with her this morning, and understandably, she's concerned.

After lunch, Kristin and Leslie ask me to help them shop for beads for the Children's Cancer Foundation Leslie works for in Nevada. While I'm not sure why I got the reputation as a good negotiator, I'm happy to help.

At 6'3" fellow cancer survivor Jeff is sturdy like an oak tree. He has Kenny Roger's beard and Michael McDonald's hair with a warm smile and twinkling green eyes. He doesn't want us to go alone so our small group heads out. We make quick stops, occasionally dipping into a shop if the bead lead seems promising.

Eventually, we walk into a tiny sliver of a shop where a small man asks us to follow him. We exit a tiny door in the rear of into yet a smaller room that feels like a cave. Jeff can't stand upright so he waits out front. This tiny space feels like the inside of a clay oven, full of bins of beads with a small lamp as the only light source.

Leslie and Kristin rummage through beads until they find what they want. Then it's my turn and I ask the vendor, "How much per bead?" He names a price that seems reasonable, for *one* bead. But Leslie and Kristin want a hundred. I introduce the idea of a volume discount and Leslie takes over.

On the way back to the hotel, we pass a Chevrolet dealership on a corner. It doesn't have a parking lot and there's only one car in the showroom. Instead of a sidewalk, a gutted trench circles the block. I ask aloud to no one in particular, "What the hell are they gonna do if I want to take a test drive?"

Michael, a 44-year-old colon cancer survivor is sitting behind me on the bus. He slaps me on the back, "You're funny, Suzanne."

The back slap startles me, "*Crap* Michael, thanks, I think."

He states the obvious, "You make me laugh."

Michael has a wife and two children in Seattle. He's also an accomplished attorney in a large and prestigious company, but at times he acts like a character from "South Park." The male adolescent part of my humor connects with him so I dig him a lot.

When we get to the hotel, I crash on my bed while Ruth showers, dresses, unpacks, repacks, flosses, and does yoga. When she's done, I get up and follow her to the dinner in the hotel.

Towards the end, I slip out and ask a clerk for an ATM. He points outside the hotel, "It's just through the perimeter gate, then around the corner to there."

I thought the ATM was in the hotel. I spent much more money than I'd anticipated, but I aided Kathmandu's economy today. I need money and walk across the driveway to the gate. The light ends on the other side where the street begins. If I go beyond this parameter, I'm going out at night alone. I hear Martha, "Don't go out at night alone. Promise me." I hear Emma, "You *better* listen to her, Mama. You don't know *everything*." I make an about-face with the belief I can get money in the morning.

On my way back to the room, there's a flurry of activity in the hall. I missed the announcement after dinner that we have to cut our duffle bag's weight from 50 to 30 pounds for a short flight in the morning. Because I've purposefully limited my knowledge of the itinerary, I only know that the short flight takes us to the beginning of the trail we'll trek for the next two weeks.

The crampons and ice pick weigh several pounds, and my boots and gear are several more. As I lighten my load, I gamble on which items I can leave behind. Everyone takes turns weighing their duffle bag on a primitive device the bellhop holds. When each bag is accepted, the bellhop ties a strand of white or red ribbon to it, giving a matching one to its owner. Ruth and I both get red ribbons.

Ruth's traveled extensively and has brought a one-stop Canteen with her. Her food and supplements weigh close to ten pounds, but they're a trekker's gold mine. Ruth comes up with a *wonderful awful* idea: "We can stuff the rest up my left sleeve and I'll use the beef jerky sticks to fill the left-handed glove."

We crack-up and I swear to her, "This is genius! And really, what's worst that can happen?" I stop laughing. "Hey Ruth, what if airport security doesn't realize how funny we are and decides to make an example out of us?" We nix the mission.

It's almost 1:00 a.m. and we're due in the lobby in three and a half hours. I need my brain to turn off but the day keeps replaying itself over and over in my mind. I can't stop wondering, "Is *this* Bob Seger's Kathmandu?"

In Durbar Square, Kathmandu, Nepal

Maju Deval Temple - "Hippy Temple" in Durbar Square

Swayambhunath Temple - "Monkey Temple"

Temple of Pashupatinath - Hindu are cremating the dead

This may have been my stalker monkey

Bikal looking across the Bagmati River

Boudhanath Temple

# 11

## I'd Rather Be Doing Stand-Up, Naked
### *(Flying into the World's Most Dangerous Airport)*

We stand outside the Kathmandu airport while the roosters still sleep. It's 5:00 a.m. and pitch dark, but for some reason, we have to fly out early—to avoid clouds, or crowds, or clowns, or *something*. I think it was clouds. There's a saying around here, "Never fly in the clouds in Nepal. The clouds have mountains in them."

Waiting outside for the airport to open, I hear an excited voice behind me, "I can't believe we're flying into Lukla, this is crazy!"

I look to see who lied, turn and croak, "Lukla?" I'm begging the voice to correct me.

The response is giddy, "Yes! Isn't this crazy?!"

Lukla? *The most dangerous airport in the world*, Lukla! No *fucking* way!

The destination is confirmed and I hear the absentee Charlie Wittmack in my head, "… at least you don't have to fly to Lukla …blah, blah, blah. *The most dangerous airport* in the world, blah, blah, blahbiddy, blah."

My head reverberates from the explosion of *my worst imaginable nightmare*, "Oh my god, no way! No *stupid* way! I am *not* flying into the most dangerous airport in the world!" Shock and terror leave me momentarily speechless. Lights dim, and sounds become hollow and funneled. It's time for fight or flight, and I'm a fighter, but I have nothing nor anyone to fight. I'm barely audible, "I'm gonna kill Charlie Wittmack."

More than one person wonders why I want to hurt Charlie. I know it's not fair to blame him. It's not his fault I didn't read the itinerary … it's Martha's fault! Oh my god I feel dizzy.

The repetition of the word Lukla caused people's energy to shift and skyrocket. My stomach is so upset by the time I get through security to the gate, I *really* have to use the bathroom. I slam the bathroom stall closed to find there's no toilet paper. Not even a toilet paper holder. Aww, geez almighty!

I make a beeline to the airport kiosk and report the oversight. The clerk informs me, "No, you use *your* paper."

"*My* paper? What paper?"

"You buy paper." He points to packets of toilet paper for sale and I nod and say, "Yes please!" I put a wad of rupees on the counter and flee. I'm in a hell of a hurry.

Back at the gate, everyone mills about chatting until Justin announces, "It's time to go." He sees me recoil and approaches me. "No Justin! I'm not ready to go. Honestly dude, I may not be going. In fact, *I'm probably not* going."

He grins and ushers me outside to the three waiting shuttle buses. I slowly board my assigned color, the red one and slide into the seat next to Ang Lhakpa. I greet her, "Namaste" and she does the same, but her greeting seems forced. Her face has an unnatural hue and her anxiety is registering with mine.

She walks from her home in the Khumbu valley to Lukla once a month, to take a flight to Kathmandu to get her blood work checked. She knows the dangers of this flight all too well, and she's obviously not happy about this one. I know she and Lhakpa are devout Buddhists, but she's *nowhere close to Zen.*

Unexpectedly, Justin boards and asks Ruth to switch buses, and flights, with him. She's being moved to the white ribbon bus and I want to know why. Why her and not me, or him, or her? Everybody knows it's bad luck to make changes during a big game and this flight is Super-Bowl big.

I do a quick evaluation of the remaining passengers on the bus and estimate their karma. This *looks* like an honest, morally upright group that deserves to live. Two of the sixteen seats on the plane belong to Clergy. In addition to Father Frank, Reverend Richard is on our plane. He's a 55-year-old Episcopal priest and cancer survivor with an offbeat and intelligent sense of humor. I haven't interacted with him directly, but he's made me laugh out loud several times. I think to myself, "I happily take the two clergies over the four doctors. Dear Lord, I hope we don't need a doctor."

The three planes carrying our group are so small they're relegated to the outskirts of the airport. They're so far from the terminal we're have to get shuttled to them. The further out we go, the smaller the planes get. They go from small, to smaller, to tiny, to finally the ones the Nepalese admit are *teensy.*

Justin points, "We're here!"

I follow his finger and my heart crashes, "Oh my god, it's not like the smallest worst-case commuter plane I'd imagined; it's in *that* plane's toy box!"

When our buses don't stop, I swat at Justin, "That's not funny!"

He's happy to be wrong but as soon as he starts to apologize, his eyes become transfixed and he stutter-stops. I look to see what's distracted him and see three *planelettes* waiting for us.

My heart and stomach high-five each other trading places. The photo of me taken when I see our "airplanes" is spot on. I look absolutely sickened.

Someone on the bus comments they can't believe I'm really this nervous. My eyes are watering yet I doubt I'll ever blink again.

Someone else defends me, "She's not kidding. She's really afraid right now." It's Father Frank.

John tries to empathize with my fear by sharing a personal one, his extreme fear of heights. His seats at Minnesota Vikings football games are on the highest deck and his family goes ahead of him, allowing him to summit at his own pace. Misery born of fear loves company, but he's not afraid of flying, so he'll have to wait until we get to the mountains, *if* we make it there.

When we arrive I notice how closely the buses have parked to the planes. Maybe they're trying to prevent runners. I know I want to run. I mean I *really* want to run. I don't know what to do and for the first time in my life, I may actually flee. If I do run, I'm gonna *Usain Bolt* this bitch.

Ang Lhakpa assured me more than once on our short ride that she's fine, but as soon as we step off the bus, she runs behind it and throws up. As I step out of line to offer assistance, Lhakpa appears at her side.

I pray in earnest, "Oh dear God, please help us all. *The Buddhists are hurling.*"

After a few steps I reach the plane and consciously will my right foot to the "step-up ladder." But that foot isn't doing anything my brain doesn't give it permission to do, and like our Tibetan trekking passes, there's a hold on it.

My instincts are usually spot on and they're warning me that something horrific is going to happen. The flying nightmares must have been premonitions – a fatal plane crash is going to happen.

My thoughts compete for attention and I have to organize and prioritize them in an instant. The processing is visual, kinesthetic, auditory, and at light speeds, using all senses at once. Strangely enough, emotion is now largely absent. I'm in serious adult therapist mode:

**Option One.** Stay in Kathmandu for two weeks without knowing a soul, then come up with a boatload of money to pay for it. I can learn to panhandle.

**Plan B.** God does something magical, *immediately*. I figure I wouldn't be in this situation in the first place if *Someone* was paying closer attention, so, yeah, time for a miracle blessing.

**Number Three.** *Bam*, I see my daughter Emma's face. I sense her pride in me and in what I'm doing, and I know without a doubt, "There's *no way* I'm letting her down." I have to role-model courage although I feel like passing out. No matter the outcome, I won't dare pass up an opportunity, no, make that a *responsibility*, to role-model to a role-model. I'm *crazy proud* of Emma Claire.

**The Conclusion.** "Suzanne, you came halfway around the world to do this thing, so put your big girl panties on and get your ass on that plane. Stop holding up the line."

I pray fast and hard and respectfully bottom line it, "I'm Your child and this is Your plane, so, whatever happens, it's on You. I'm O.K. with that."

Even though I still feel doom, I get on the plane. It's shockingly tiny, with only eight rows, one seat on each side, and two up front for the pilots – which by the way you can see! I don't want to see the drivers. I'll misinterpret every move they'll make as the one the black box will focus on.

Mary told me at the hotel that she and John asked to be on separate flights, but they're both on this one. I point at John and ask, "Hey, what's he doing here?" She says, "Oh well. They probably overlooked it, but it's fine."

"No, it's not. It's not *fine*. *Nothing* about this flight is *fine*. Besides Mary, do you know what *fine* stands for? As a previous drug and alcohol counselor, I do. It stands for – **F**ucked up, **I**nsecure, **N**eurotic, and **E**mpty. So I guess *it is* **FINE**.

"We just don't want to make a deal out of it."

"I'll be sure to tell your orphaned children how accommodating you were. They'll be so proud." I point at Leslie, "She's not on the same flight with Kristin." I point at Andy and see his Dad Brian across the aisle from him, "Well here's a son and father, and obviously they're O.K. with it." I quickly move on to the seat behind Brian, and point at Lhakpa. My finger moves to the seat behind Lhakpa and there sits his wife, Ang Lhakpa, which means more parents on the same plane. Mary sees them and grins. In a sharp whisper I warn her of my earlier observation, "I wouldn't get too cocky because *the Buddhist are hurling*. I say we get off and regroup."

I choose to think of these treasured people as an insurance policy. There's no way God would let anything happen to *this* plane. Right? I re-tally the goodness of the group and feel satisfied. Man oh man, I hope no one has skeletons.

I notice Ang Lhakpa's head lowered with hands in prayer. She's praying her *ass off*. She's made this flight so many times, but *on this particular one*, she seems scared. In front of her, Lhakpa sits staring forward in a daze.

This is a horrible sign and I fear the next one I see will be from God and read, "*Welcome!*"

Well I'm here and I'm doing this, so I'm either gonna keep it together, or lose my shit and require sedation and restraints. I really need to be unconscious right now. How can I make myself pass out just long enough to …?

Someone tugs my sleeve and I turn to find Mary's hand extended toward me in a fist. She wants to give me something and I give her my palm. In the center she places a small stone engraved with, "Hope." *Not* "Certainty" *or* "Knowing" …just good old, "Hope." I thank Mary for getting me stoned and she laughs.

A flight attendant comes down the aisle carrying a tray of cotton balls and candy. The cotton balls are for your ears against the engines' noise, and the candy is to cause you to swallow to keep your ears unstopped.

Father Frank sat beside me from Detroit to Amsterdam so he knows the intensity of my fear. He switches seats with Jeff so he can sit beside me and he asks if there's anything he can do.

I'm resolute, "Yes please. With all that's Right and Holy, punch me in the head so hard you knock me out."

He can't be baited or bought and replies, "Would you take a prayer instead?"

"If that's your final offer. But can we make it a group thing?" Everyone gathers round and I ask Father Frank, "Will you please include that whole ' …and keep Your cheek close to Suzanne's part again? I really liked that."

He smiles, remembering, and shakes his head. We all hold hands while he prays.

In those few final seconds before takeoff, I pray one last time and a tad more specifically,

"Dear God, *I'm asking as hard as I can. Please* keep these planes safe using *every* Guardian Angel of *every* soul on board. And, I'd *really* appreciate it if I could remember this flight for something *besides* turbulence and terror. Amen."

I've never been in a plane this small, so I have nothing to compare it to. As the engines race, the volume grows and the plane shakes at an impossible level. Right before it explodes, it lurches forward and we're airborne.

The weather is close to perfect. The sunrise blankets the city in warm yellows and oranges, giving me a different view of Kathmandu. I'm able to see greater expanses while the entire city shrinks and this time, disappears.

Cityscapes, no matter how exotic, are still man-made and therefore limited, but now, we're flying into terrain untouched by man. The landscape I'm trying to comprehend is almost impossible to describe, at least with my vocabulary. I *can* tell you, I feel immense awe, *completely incompatible* with fear.

My thoughts have stopped racing, but the view catches my breath over and over. At times, I have to look up to see the tops of these mountains while also looking down to see the clouds. The view runs off the page; it goes until it's just not there.

Almost everything I've ever seen, is disproportionate to *anything* I'm seeing now.

But on this day and on this flight, there is *zero* turbulence. Are we gliding? Justin sits in front of me and his smile affirms, this is a great plane ride.

He rests his forehead on the window and begins, "Glorious are you, Lord, more majestic than the everlasting mountains. How beautiful on the mountains are the feet of those who bring good news. God saw all that He had made and, indeed, it was very good." Tears and mucous stream unchecked down my face.

We fly over luscious greens mountains into uninhabitable snow-capped ones within fifteen minutes. I tap Justin on the shoulder, "Please say all that again."

He begins anew, "Glorious are you, Lord, more majestic …"

Pure peace and gratitude connect me to everything and everyone, all at once. This flight is better than every amazing flying dream I've ever had. Well that, times a million and then another million!

In my best dreams, I fly Superman style over the most gorgeous landscapes imaginable. My favorite destination is the Caribbean Islands where water is crystal clear and blue, and white sandy beaches host the greenest palm trees I've ever seen. I often tell people I'm certain reincarnation is real because I was a palm tree in a previous happy life. In these dreams, I fly with ease, and without fear.

I'm having an *unbelievable* experience, but Justin can't leave well enough alone. He's made this flight before so he knows what I'm about to see. He taps impatiently on my knee, leans back and points between the pilots. All I see is a mountain wall.

Justin's excited, "Look … there, it's Lukla!"

I see a tiny village built smack up a mountain's ass. I'm struck by the absurdity of building a village here and wonder how the idea ever took off.

But I haven't reacted yet, so Justin thrusts his finger forward again. Then I see it, the so-called landing strip. It looks like a toothpick from here and we're *way* too high to land on it.

He yells above the engine noise, "It's the runway! Do you see it?"

Yes, I see it and now I understand why this is the most dangerous airport in the world. I get why all the accidents end in fatalities. On one end of the runway is a vertical mountain face, on the other is a cliff with a 900 ft. drop off.

Our plane descends rapidly and somehow, I now understand geometry and the need for math skills. This little plane has to dive – no drop – quickly enough to get in position to ascend upward. The landing strip is small and void of forgiveness. There's *zero* opportunity for a second pass. The pilot makes the landing, or the news.

Again, I swat at Justin and beg him with only my face, "Why?"

It doesn't matter because fear parachuted somewhere between take off and, "Am I dreaming, who else sees this?"

As we get closer, the pilots press buttons while turning knobs and rotating hand-cranks above their heads. I'm sure we're way too high. They furiously turn more handles and the plane suddenly drops. The noise is a deafening silence, and we free fall a few seconds. The vibrations and noises resume and our approach is from below the runway, at the absolute perfect angle and speed. The plane lands on *feathers*.

What an amazing and terrifying magic trick. And I never want to do it again.

During the spontaneous applause, Justin kicks us off, "For they are Jolly Good *Pilots.*"

The pilots shake their heads knowingly. This ain't their first rodeo but I'll tell you what, it's my first and last. I don't ever want to do that again.

The door opens and I exit the plane into a place that's bigger than life. I'm in the freakin' Himalayan Mountains, and the best part is, *I'm free of **all** my fears!*

Que the Doobie Brothers … *"What a Fool Believes."*

At the Kathmandu Airport while the roosters still sleep

The moment I see our tiny plane with Ang Lhakpa

Our Tiny Plane

L-R Jeff, Rev. Richard, Father Frank, Mary, Brian, Kay, Me, Justin, Leslie. Not shown John, and Photo by Andy

Lhakpa and Ang Lhakpa

Lukla Airport

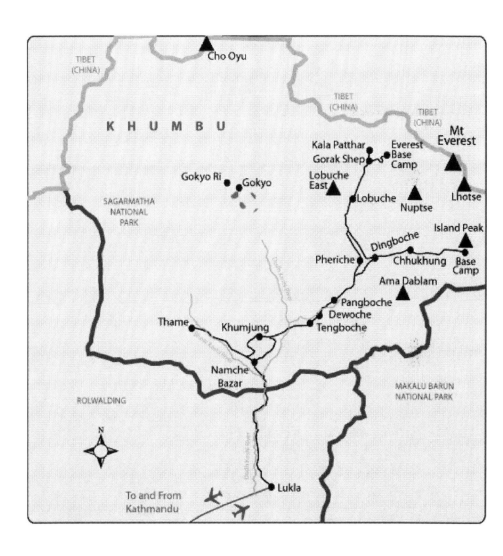

Lukla to Imja Tse (Island Peak) map

# 12

## Piece of Cake

*(Trek to Phakding—8,562 ft.)*

The landing at Tenzing-Hillary airport is spectacular, and more importantly, unspectacular. Lukla is considered the "Gateway to the Himalayas" because the primary trail to Everest begins here. It takes two weeks of hard trekking to get to this point without flying from Kathmandu, so Lukla is a necessary evil for some, a joy ride for others. The tiny village carved into a mountain is where the rubber meets the road; except there is no *rubber*, because there are no roads.

Homes are built on earth that has exceeded planetary expansion rules. Transportation doesn't exist outside of the two, or four-legged. From here on out there'll be few places to access the internet, and cell service will be extremely limited. I'm ready because I went off the grid when I flew out of Charlotte. *I'm being* **all in**.

The air has changed from sea level to over 9,000 ft. becoming super crisp and clean. Lukla's extreme incline creates amazing views over the crater-sized valleys below. The air is perfumed in lush shades of green.

Main Street is paved with the same stone and brick that construct the short buildings. The street is narrow and we have to step to the side when yak approach. Yak look like fancy, foreign buffalo and I've heard they're sensitive to human's suffering. If that's true, they deserve a better sounding name than *yak*.

The tearoom is on the far side of the village and upon arrival I see our luggage has already arrived. Asian Trekking is providing Sherpas, porters, and kitchen staff. In addition to our duffle bags, food and supplies are also being strapped on the yak.

Inside the tearoom we're offered hot tea and cookies. I don't really want any hot tea because I've yet to mature into someone who can responsibly drink hot liquids. I typically burn my tongue and can't taste anything for hours. But when in Rome or Nepal…

I ask Michael if there's any honey on his table. He picks up a red plastic container that looks like catsup and has a handmade label taped around the bottle that reads, "Honey." He sells it, "Yeah, it must be. It's heavy like honey too."

I can't imagine why honey would turn up in a catsup bottle, but when he extends it to me, I take it. The tape *does* say honey, so I up-end it and squeeze. A projectile of catsup explodes into the shallow cup, assaulting the clear tea.

Michael thinks exploding, tea curdling catsup is table-slapping funny. I freely admit to him, "I deserved that. What kind of *moron* picks up a red bottle with catsup residue on it, and believes a sticky note that says, "Honey?"

Michael assaults the table harder and after I let him get some of it out of his system, I lean over and a whisper, "But why would *you* do that to someone?"

His hands fly into the air, "No *I swear,* I thought it was honey!"

As I head to the door, Michael protests louder, "Really! I *didn't* know!"

I turn for eye contact, "O.K. mister, you just keep telling yourself that."

His laugh exposes his amusement, so I walk outside with total satisfaction.

I grab my duffle bag before it gets harnessed to a yak. I need to transfer more items into my already bulging backpack. In my vulnerability, I have the brilliant idea that more stuff = better.

Dr. Charlie stands nearby watching the fluidity and efficiency of the staff. He reports his neck and shoulder feel much better after my elbow-grinding, and he thanks me again for helping. I'm so thankful I don't have any back or neck problems in this moment. My response is hearty, "You're so welcome. No problem!"

I turn to head back up the steep steps and the weight of my boots causes me to misjudge the steps. Trekking boots take themselves way too seriously in an attempt to mirror the ground upon which they walk. Mine snags the edge of the step and plunges me forward. Forward doesn't equal upward and momentum propels me head-long into the next stair. I flail about furiously in an attempt to re-establish balance. I try to add and subtract motion to create a vertical position again.

I'm falling *up* the stairs which has to look hilarious, but when I turn and look at Dr. Charlie, he isn't on the ground laughing. In fact, he looks concerned and takes a step towards me. I bolt upright and wave him off. There has to be something wrong with this guy because he should be *howling.*

Our destination for today is the small village of Phakding. Lower in altitude than Lukla, it's mostly downhill and the path is often muddy and slippery. My backpack soon becomes heavy and I regret my last-minute idea to add items, and therefore, weight. A little further down the trail, I wonder if I can stow my backpack behind a rock and pick it up on the return.

We're in the early parts of the Khumbu Trail where everything is so lush and green, it appears to be dripping. The trail winds along the Dudh Kosi River, which creates gorgeous waterfalls. I'm most certainly in the foothills of heaven. The scenery is breathtaking and I don't want to miss a single sight. I don't want anyone else to miss one either, so I point out vistas, saying, "Take time to smell the roses." By the end of the day, it'll become a directional finger pointing, "Roses."

At a mid-morning break, Kristin feels terrible. She can't breathe and trekking requires a lot of that. I ask her if she's ever done a "Nettie Pot" and Leslie assures me she has *not*. She encourages Kristin to try it so I pour salt into two cups of very warm water the porters recently boiled, and we walk out of sight to the side of a building. I tilt my cup to show her how to inhale salt water. She grasps the concept of nasal irrigation when she sees me blow brown trail dust and mucus out. She inhales two rounds of salt water and is thrilled to breathe through her nose again.

The terrain is often straight up or down, always requiring a strict focus on footing. Jeff and I have been walking together and I ask him how he's doing. He's winded and takes an extra-large inhale before announcing, "I'm living the dream. Yep, livin' the dream."

I slowed down a long time ago and mirror his sentiment, "Yeah, we've both lost a little piss and vinegar since the good old days."

Jeff reminisces, "The first time I saw you was in Detroit when you were signing for a big bottle of Vodka. It was love at first sight."

"For me, or the vodka?" Jeff laughs easily, and this time, especially heartily. I typically have the best connections with people that think I'm funny. Usually, it's with those that get my off-handed observations.

This morning has gone pretty good so there's only one thing bothering me more than fatigue right now, and it's Justin. Bless his little heart, he's officially on my nerves. But the flight to Lukla made me love him, so when he continues to confuse Alabama and Arkansas, I stay tolerant.

He lived in Arkansas for ten favorable months of his 28-year-old life, and he wants to reconnect with that happy time. He thinks Arkansas and Alabama are both "hillbilly." He keeps asking me to say something hillbilly. I assure him *I don't speak hillbilly*.

When we get to the first of several suspension bridges we'll have to use to cross over the river, my first thought is disconcerting. "Why would anyone TP a bridge?" In the south, TP-ing is somewhat of a finger flip, while in the north, it's done to welcome new neighbors. As I get closer I realize it's not toilet paper. It's hundreds of long white prayer flags flying confidently in the wind. I dig this praying, meditating, and being grateful country. I'm moved and humbled by it.

John has taken post at this end of this crossway, conjuring up the courage to pass. This is an unfair test for someone with a fear of heights. While Lukla was both unfair and *cruel* for someone with a fear of flying, I'm safely on the ground now. I offer to wait with him but he declines. He has to get to his seat in Viking Stadium on his own.

Justin and I step onto the bridge and into the wind. Justin, comfortable and confident, quickly arrives in the middle of the bridge. He stops to wait for me and as soon as I get close enough I see the "cat that ate the canary" grin on his face. He goads, "Look over. I'll do it with you. Look *way* over."

I hold the rail to look down, but without bending forward. When Justin leans full tilt boogie into the rail, he causes the bridge to sway, and me to fall forward. My heart lunges into my throat, and I chide him, "Oh my god, what the hell is wrong with you?! You're like a big puppy; be still big dummy!" My heart is pounding *its heart* out as he laughs and repeats a variation on a theme, "I like you Suzanne. I think we can be friends."

I lean slightly over the rail to look far below. The first thing I see is our documentarian, John Richard, loaded for bear with cameras. He's on the edge of the river bank which seems unlikely. I look back to the side of the mountain to retrace our approach to the bridge. I'm sure, we were never close enough to the river to safely get to its banks, so how did he do it? He's carrying at least thirty pounds of heavy equipment to boot. I've heard stories about John Richard's toughness on past A+BC trips.

A year ago an A+BC group climbed Mt. Kilimanjaro and on the way up, John Richard got an abscessed tooth, replete with infection and fever. Instead of ending his trip, he insisted that one of the doctors pull it, which they did – *without* Novocain – **Bam!** True story.

By now I'm leaning all the way over while looking upward at the sky. I hear equal measures of river and wind and I'm ecstatic. I feel like I'm dreaming and I want to fly. I push my arms straight out and yell to Justin, "I always fly Superman style!"

He leans into the rail with me, extends his arms too, and yells, "Superman!"

I echo him, "Yeah! *Super*man!"

I want to be able to recall this moment forever — how the air feels and smells, the colors of the mountains, river, and sky, the raw energies of happiness and love. But the mood shifts as soon as we step off the bridge when Justin starts again, "Hey, Suzanne, go on and say something hillbilly."

"Dude! What is your *biggest* problem? Yes, Alabama and Arkansas are both southern states that start with the letter 'A', but Justin, they are *not* the same and I'm from *Ala freakin' bama*. We have gentlemen, rednecks, country-boys, and the occasional asshole, but we *don't* have hillbillies."

Now he's dissecting, "So what do you call country-boy rednecks?"

"Good ol' boys. We call 'em good ol' boys."

"Naw, *I'd* call 'em hillbillies."

"Well yes, *you* would, because you're an *idiot*."

His amusement explodes, "I think we can be good friends!"

Man, he's lucky he's so stinkin' adorable!

It's been a long morning by the time we arrive for lunch, but I have no idea what time it is, or how far we've come. Details are becoming irrelevant. Lunch in a structure built high off the ground so it feels like a tree house with tables and chairs. From this spot, we can see the green valley dipping far below us and rising far above us. We're suspended in a green paradise.

I stow my backpack under the table and when I look up, Justin's sitting across from me waving, "Hey, Suzanne!" I like Justin and think he's a doll, but maybe we could use some time apart?

Dr. Deming is on Justin's right and greets me also. I haven't interacted directly with him since our first meeting with my big bottle of vodka in Detroit. Oh boy, I'm getting a do-over, a second chance to make a good first impression. No way will I blow it again (That's what she said!).

As we eat, Dr. Deming shows interest in me, asking thoughtful questions, and more importantly, by listening to me. I want to have a conversation with him, but Justin won't stop interrupting, "Yeah, Doc, she's from Alabama. She's a *hill*billy. Hey Suzanne, *say something **hillbilly**.*"

I've told him *umpteen* times to drop it but he won't, and he's blowing my second chance. I lean over and *hissper*, "If you don't shut your face, I'm going to punch you in your tiny nut sack."

His toothy grin launches his goofy laugh, "We're gonna be good friends!"

Having been raised in the south, I was taught that certain things are expected and non-negotiable. I say "sir" and "ma'am" and I'm respectful to those in authority. Being good and doing right was expected, and you didn't get a reward or a cookie for doing what you were supposed to do. We were taught manners and expected to use them. Another widely accepted truth is that cursing is wrong, probably a sin, so kids don't curse. Adults, however, are allowed to curse if sufficiently provoked by a dumbass. But, respect is always priority, so I hold my tongue.

But sometime between the soup and the best grilled cheese and tomato sandwich I've ever had, Justin goes too far. He blurts out, "I used to live in the South so *I know* what it sounds like. Go on Suzanne, *say something hillbilly!*"

"O.K., I've got some hillbilly for you Justin."

Everything about him screams anticipation and approval for whatever I'm about to say so I give it to him, "O.K., here's your hillbilly. 'How about, *shut the fuck up Justin.*' Is *that* hillbilly enough for you?"

He starts applauding after the profanity, "I knew it! I knew it Suzanne! You and I are *definitely* gonna be good friends!"

I start to high-five him and notice a third person laughing. I *flinch* knowing that I didn't *just curse*, I used the eff word! No matter how gracious this Dr. Deming may be, I will *not* get a third chance.

After lunch we resume trekking and shortly approach what must be a mirage. It's a beautiful teen-aged girl with wavy long dark hair. Her facial features are more Asian than Nepali, so I assume she's not from here. She's standing at the edge of a cliff, playing a violin. The music resonates above the river with a backdrop of lush green rhododendron, magnolia and pine trees. Waterfalls create random and vertical movement behind her. The whole scene seems surreal.

A man I assume is her father stands in front of her with a video camera. He's capturing this moment and can watch it again and again. I want to re-experience it too and I stare, almost transfixed, as her body moves as an extension of her violin. The violin is playing her, *not* the other way around, and she cooperates fully.

After another couple of hours on difficult terrain, I'm told we're getting close to tonight's lodging in Phakding. We start walking through a single lane village and pass a group of good-looking guys sitting outside, drinking beer and having a good time. They're clearly having fun while I'm tired as hell, and I may stink, somebody does. I make a general announcement, "Not to be rude, but I'm gonna take five, or an hour and five, over here with this group. But don't worry, I'll be home for dinner."

I don't know who calls me, but it's someone at the end of the buildings, and they want me to see what's beyond them. When I get to them I can see Phakding in the distance, but it doesn't look real. The small village is nestled on the other side of the river and built of varying sized structures, with mostly blue roofs. It's a stunning postcard view that can only be accessed via another long suspension bridge. I want to go to there, so I keep moving.

At the bridge's entrance, John stands contemplating the crossing. This bridge is long, but not particularly high, so the river feels more alive. Once again, he declines my offer to stay with him.

I'm entirely grateful for this bridge because without it, I'd need a big stork or a cannon. Reverend Richard and I cross together singing loudly enough for John to hear, "John'll be comin' round the mountain when he comes (echo) when he comes. He'll be …"

We arrive under an archway that leads down a grassy area, back to the river. The single storied lodging lines both sides of the lawn. Since this is our first night on the trail, I don't realize these rooms are the Himalayas' Ritz Carlton. Our room has two single beds, a toilet, *and* a shower.

The teahouse sits at the lawn's end by the river. Tables and chairs sit between the lodges and Justin is already kicked-back playing his guitar when we arrive. I plop nearby and start taking off my boots. Teresa walks over and hands me a red floppy hat that reads, "Nepal – Top of the World." She tells me, "I bought this for you in the last village because with your fair skin, you'll fry under the Himalayan sun."

My knee-jerk reaction is to pay her for it, but I hear Mu in my head, "Floss, when someone gives you something, just accept it and say thank you, otherwise you'll take away their happy. Don't ever take away someone's happy."

I'm touched Teresa thought of me and bought a hat for me. I sincerely thank her and think, "Wow, she's really good at this compassion thing."

I go to my room to find my duffle bag waiting on me. Ruth has already unpacked so I step outside while I wait for my turn to shower. Leslie and Kristin are in front of our room tying their prayer flags together, and I offer to help. As I hold one end of the strand and Leslie holds the other, Kristin takes pictures of the personalized flags in between.

After I shower I head to the Tea House for dinner. Dr. Charlie diverts me to where he's relaxing in the grass courtyard, reiterating his appreciation for the muscle relief. I know it was just this morning, but it feels like days ago. He continues by giving not so subtle hints that he'd be mighty grateful, if I could do it *just* one more time, *please*? Showing compassion, I grind my elbow into the crook of his neck until the whining stops.

Several people aren't at dinner and I'm not surprised. This level of exertion isn't normal and it's taking a toll on many of us. We began taking our Diamox this morning for altitude sickness, but nausea has a head start. I think of my cancer doctor and wish for his magic pill.

The morning of my third round of chemotherapy my oncologist was honest, "Chemo can have a cumulative effect. How are you doing with nausea?"

"It's a little rough, but I'm not throwing up." Throwing up is my gauge as to whether or not I'm dying, so I'm fine.

He stepped closer to the examination table, bent forward, and in a quieter voice, asked me, "Have you ever smoked pot?"

I was caught off guard but didn't break eye contact. My first thought, "Is this a trick question?" was followed by "What's with the creepy drug dealer vibe?"

I admit, "Yes, when I was younger, and it was *legal.*"

He chuckled but stayed in his role, "O.K., I've got something for you called Marinol. After today's chemo, go home and take one, get a big bowl of ice cream, sit on the couch, and listen to "The Grateful Dead.""

*What!* I was stoked— getting pot in a pill! This dude was awesome! I thought I might love the big lug.

On the way home, I filled the prescription and stocked up at the grocery store. After I took a pill, I sat and waited for its effects. After about ten minutes, I noticed the nausea had subsided. After fifteen minutes, I was hungry. At the twenty-minute mark I ordered pizza, and after thirty minutes, I was on the phone making sure everything was ok. I wanted to high-five the delivery guy a long time ago.

As it turns out, the THC (creates the high) is taken out of Marinol, so there was no high. What there was, was, an unquenchable hunger from *a thousand hells.* I ate everything and all the time. Brad called me every morning around ten and interrupted my second lunch.

My job became fulltime hunter-gatherer, which created endless trips to the grocery store. I blew up to over 200 pounds, so I purposely didn't wear a wig or scarf when grocery shopping. My appearance made the declaration, "Don't judge me, I have big problems. My doctor is trying to *almost* kill me."

    Our first evening on the trail I eat very little dinner and go directly to bed. The last thing I remember before falling asleep is acknowledging the obvious, *this trip will **not** be a piece of cake.*

National Luminary Pasang Lhamu Memorial Gate Entering the Khumbu Valley

Yak

A study in contrast

The girl and the violin

Entering Phakding

With Kelly in the courtyard after a very long day

Lhakpa introducing the Sherpa in Phakding

The prayer flag project

# 13

## It Only Hurts When I'm Conscious
*(Trek to Namche Bazar—11,286 ft.)*

At 6:00 a.m. Ruth opens the door to porters serving hot tea and honey as a wake-up call. We serenade them, "Tea for two, and two for tea. Me for you, and you for me."

The tea service lasts throughout the trek. Singing at six a.m. lasts two more days.

During breakfast, we learn it's one of the caregiver's birthday. She shares her birthday wish firmly, "It's simple. For today, I don't want to hear anyone ask how much further we have to go. Don't ask the Sherpa, and don't talk about it to each other. Be in the moment."

Well that sounds reasonable enough, but since I do *not* want to be a rule-breaker, I raise my hand. "O.K., we're not allowed to ask, 'How much further?' But can we ask, 'How far have we come?'" The room explodes in laughter then implodes into silence when we hear the answer. It's an *emphatic*, "**No**."

In the courtyard, Judith leads us in Qigong. She's a Social Psychology Professor at Drake University where she specializes in stereotyping and prejudice, ethnic conflict and peace-making, and theories of consciousness. She's fabulous and I'm intrigued by her.

After Dr. Deming's meditation, the Sherpa are introduced, with their highly impressive climbing resumes.

Afterward, we're divided into three groups, each with a doctor and a lead Sherpa. The groups depart ten minutes apart; I'm in the first one, the Red Pandas. Our group's doctor for the day is Leah, a 42-year-old cancer survivor and oncologist from Wisconsin. She's intelligent, sweet, a little quiet, and laughs easily as we walk. I try to imagine what she'd be like as my oncologist because she's the complete opposite from mine.

We're facing a 2,000 ft. increase in altitude to our next stop, Namche Bazaar. We're warned it'll be a hard trek. Often the path is too narrow to walk side by side, as it winds over rocky and irregular terrain, many with dangerous to *deadly* drop-offs. A millisecond of being slightly off-balance can tip momentum downward and take you over the edge.

For a long time, I've sensed someone walking closely behind me, and closer still to the path's edge. I step to the side to allow the person to pass, but the footsteps fall silent with mine. Assuming my snail's pace is acceptable, I continue forward and when my foot slips, I start to fall. *Instantly* I'm supported, stabilized, and held upright. I spin to thank the one who rescued me from a certain fall, but no one's there.

There is a Sherpa *several* feet behind me, pausing and enjoying the scenery. He's way too far to have helped me, but there's absolutely no one else around us. I have to ask, "Was that you?" He makes brief eye contact with a bashful smile and nods that it was.

"But how did you get from …to here …to..?" I point at the space *between* us. "You couldn't have."

His expression tells me that he's used to being accused of helping people in sudden, unanticipated, and lifesaving situations – like that's part of his job.

My adrenaline is still pumping and I grab his hand, "Thank you dude."

I'm still marveling, "You may have just saved my life, so really, *dhanyabad* ("thank you" in Nepalese) so much." He laughs but I wonder if he's just being polite, or does he *really* get my humor?

I introduce myself and when I tell him my name, he repeats it spot-on the first time. I'm impressed, "Oh, so you've met another Suzanne!"

"No, you're the first, but Suzanne is a good name."

When I ask his name, I repeat to him, "Lindsey." He doesn't correct me, but when I hear another Sherpa call his name, I realize I'm wrong. I have him repeat it several more times, and it morphs from "Lindsey" to "Lendzing" to finally "Tenzing." Another smile, and I know I've finally got it. He has a contagious smile that *always* includes his eyes.

He understands English better than he speaks it, although he speaks it well. He's able to communicate volumes with facial expressions. Sometimes words are meager and sometimes they interfere, but communication with Tenzing is always easy.

He's from the same village as Lhakpa where children are named based on the day of the week they're born. There are three Tenzings on the Asian Trekking staff. I learn he has a wife and four children that live a three-hour walk from where we'll be tonight.

I try to empathize with him, "It must be hard being away from home and your family." He doesn't seem to understand because I'm validating feelings he *doesn't* have.

"I'll see my family tonight."

I'm thrilled for him, "That's nice they can come see you."

"No, I'll be home tonight."

I'm bummed and tell him so, "Man, I sure wish you were going all the way with us. Hey, Tenzing, remember that time you saved my life?"

He laughs and nods up and down until his head changes directions, "No, I'll be back in the morning."

I'm incredulous. "Wait, how?"

"I'll walk home and back, no big deal. I'll be back before you wake up."

God almighty is he crazy? He's gonna make this three hour trip in the freaking Himalayan Mountains, IN THE DARK! I'm entirely speechless. I'm not sure if he's kidding or crazy, but I know he's sincere.

I'm gonna miss him, and I'll pull for a speedy recovery.

After the group takes a short rest I walk with Marilyn and her bum ankle. She's a 56-year-old caregiver from Iowa and we bonded in Kathmandu over our *inability* to blend in. With reddish hair, blue eyes and freckles, we stick out. She's lagging further and further behind, and I'm digging the slower pace. O.K., I *need* the slower pace. Some of these people are in crazy good shape, but not me so I'm the first to admit, "I undertrained."

The trail is so narrow we have to stand to the side on any available space to let the yak pass. I notice these animals often have to be redirected when they get near Marilyn. They look at her with their huge bovine eyes and seem to have an understanding of human suffering, and a desire to help – or is that my imagination?

The other groups, the Snow Leopards and the Yak, have caught up with us, so we take a collective break. Teresa's portable speaker plays, *Ain't No Mountain High Enough* by Michael McDonald. I'm sitting this one out until Teresa yells, "Suzanne! Are you dancing?"

I dive into dance mode with the "Running Man." Three well-choreographed strides later I realize, "At this altitude, the Running Man is stupid. No, check that. At this altitude, *dancing* is stupid. No, check that too. At this altitude, *movement* is stupid."

Towards the end of the day the increase in altitude takes a toll on a lot of us. Marilyn is at the point of tears and requests to be left alone on the trail to *die*. I can't argue with her because I'm starting to feel weak and I need this freaking day to end.

Dr. Deming intervenes, cheering her on and giving 100% to the cause. His verbal encouragements include chanting, "One more step" with the Sherpas in Nepalese, "Ajai yek paila. Ajai yek paila. One more step. One more step."

Dr. Deming sings, dances, and then fakes a pratfall. An unsuspecting yak rounds the corner and becomes part of the routine. Deming dramatizes in slow motion getting sideswiped by the yak and bouncing off the mountain wall, then finally falling to ground. He springs to his feet in a cloud of dirt that tie dyes his white tee shirt in brown and red.

He makes me belly laugh and I'm inspired to inspire, but I'm not committed to body-sacrificing, yet. However, I want to practice his one request: that we show compassion for each other. I walk in front of Marilyn and give her the best encouragement I have available, "Come on baby girl, you got this! Ginger's Rule so let's kick this mountain's ass!"

I know she's suffering. Hell, we're *all* suffering. Everyone must constantly raise personal high-bars of endurance,

Tonight Dr. Deming writes in his daily blog,

"Marilyn trained diligently to get fit enough to be able to support her cancer-surviving friend Kim on this journey. This second day on the trail was a difficult challenge for her. The steep uphill climb into Namche was seemingly more than she could handle. Tears flowed as she tried to muster enough strength to continue.

The rest of the team became her cheerleading squad. We cheered, sang, hugged, pleaded, cajoled, pushed, pulled, and lifted, tugged and danced Marilyn up the mountain. Suzanne Link, 48, a breast cancer survivor from Alabama, walked a few feet ahead of Marilyn, gently coaxing her forward with a sweet Southern drawl, 'Come on, baby girl, if Susannah from Alabama can do it, so can you!' That remark prompted a chorus of "Oh! Susannah" from our cheerleading choir."

I don't know how far we are from Namche, nor will I ask. I'm honoring a simple birthday wish. But I wonder what song they're gonna sing to me because I'm about to need some serious motivation, or assistance. I'm not near ready to ask for help, but may God bless the first responders when I do.

I've been pounding water so I really need to winkle. We've been hoisting upward for a long time with nowhere to step off for a quick and unnoticed pee break. On my right is the mountain wall, and on my left is a *severe* drop-off. There's no easy or quick way to make it happen, but my bladder demands I try. I'll have to get far enough ahead of everyone to go off trail and out of sight.

I haul as much ass as possible and when I think I've created enough distance, I make my move. I pivot to my left and head off-trail, but before my second boot can leave the path, a Sherpa shows up from out of nowhere. Another Sherpa falls in his shadow while a third appears suddenly from the group below. I'm trying *not* to draw attention to myself but I catch *three* sets of eyes. Either I suck at a low profile, or these guys are *really* good.

I don't have much time so I tell them all, "I *really* have to go to the bathroom." I hold up one finger, "I have to go *number one*." They understand my request but they don't want me to go off the trail here. They think it's too steep so I look back down the mountain side and I know they're right. I ask, "Is there a place soon, as in just around the curve?"

They look at each other and I can tell I'm out of luck. Looking back down I see a small, flat edge, less than ten yards down and point to it, "Look! Right there! I can go there and be right back. It's safe I promise!" (As if I had a clue.)

Without words, they take swift action — mostly a zone defense. The first guy runs back up the trail, while the one from below returns to the group. The shadow Sherpa stays put, but turns and faces the mountain to give me privacy. I'm confident, "*None shall pass.*"

The Sherpa directly above me constantly checks on me because as long as I'm talking, I'm still on the *side* of the mountain. I try and make it easy for him by giving him a lot of feedback. Eventually I just start thinking out loud, somewhat, loudly, "Yes, I'm O.K. Thank you. Yep doing fine. No problems here…Why can't I unbuckle this? You're right, this is pretty steep."

I retrieve the portable urination penis from my backpack that I received as a bon voyage gift from a friend. It's supposed to allow females to pee without squatting and wetting their legs. If I tell the story of trying to use the worthless piece of shit portable pee penis, this book would have to carry a warning label due to excessive vulgar language. Suffice it to say it was a disaster.

When I'm safely back on the trail I tell them, "I feel like we all just shared a moment and I really trust you guys. So can I ask a question, and y'all won't tell on me?" Taking their amusement as a *yes*, I ask what I really want to know, "How much further do we have to go?"

They promise it's close, but it turns out a Sherpa's mile does *not* equal a real person's mile. Their five minutes aren't accurate within my time-space continuum. Everything is actually *much* further and *much* longer than they say. Right around the corner, *they say*. Right over the hill, *they say*.

When Namche Bazaar finally appears, I feel misled. The village is built into the side of a crescent-shaped mountain that angles upward at an unreasonable slope. Our lodge is near the top so we're not there yet, or even that close. I wonder, "What kind of Einstein came up with the idea to build here? It's probably the same Svengali that planted the first flag in Lukla."

The sun is making a big production of setting. The waning rays are creating a surreal backdrop in liquid watercolors, mostly dark blues, and oranges. The fading light changes the hue in the air so it feels kind of, well, yellow. After another fifteen minutes of walking straight up, the sun is much lower, so the sky reveals different colors. Varying shades of pink melt into darker reds and purples; the effect is mesmerizing.

By the time we finally arrive at the lodge, I'm weak. I go straight to the tearoom and collapse in a chair. Marilyn is sitting across the table and as her energy improves, mine tanks. She knows I struggled too, and she wants to share this victory with me. But I can't. I'm nauseous, shaky, and faint.

Dr. Deming walks over, bends down, and wraps his arms around me. He starts rocking me from side to side in wide arcs and I wonder why the room is getting dark. Why are people suddenly whispering?

He's happy and exclaims, "Way to go, Suzanne! You're a great cheerleader!"

I exhale, "O.K., thank you, but would you please stop rocking me? I think I'm about to pass out."

"Are you serious?"

"I'm *very* serious. I'm not sure, but I think my diabetes is acting up."

He lets go and stands back to look at me, "You have *diabetes*?"

"Yes, it's another late effect from cancer. I take a pill a day and it's never given me a problem."

At this point, I'm involuntarily shaking, almost spastically, and I feel cold. I hear a voice from across the room full of concern, "Oh god, look how white she is."

Dr. Deming begins to support and raise me to my feet, "Let's get you to your room so you can lie down. It's probably exhaustion." Lhakpa is already lifting me on the other side and together, they help me to my room.

The Dr. on call is a surgeon from Iowa and I feel guilty for taking her time. I promise her I'm O.K. to be left alone, but she won't leave me until the jerking stops, and *some* color returns to my face. Her casual manner assures me I'm not an imposition and she reminds me that she's doing double duty anyway. Judith's in the room next door. She began throwing up earlier today and I wonder if she feels as poorly as I do. At least I haven't thrown up so I have to be better off. Throwing up is the worst.

The diuretic in the altitude sickness pill has kicked in, and for some reason, laying down makes my bladder feel desperate. The sinks are in the hall across from my room, and the toilet is behind them. Every time I stand up, I can't hear or see for about two seconds. It takes a lot of focus to stay upright so the first few times I go to the bathroom, the doctor goes with me. The shaking spells stop shortly, so she feels comfortable enough to leave.

For the first time I notice the window between the two beds and lean on my elbows into the sill. The sun has fully set and I marvel at the beginning of the night's sky. The village is carved into the side of this mountain and I understand why it was such a ball-buster getting here.

I'm not steady enough to go to dinner, but I don't have an appetite anyway. Lhakpa checks on me and *insists* I eat. He stresses that during this entire journey, it's imperative to eat and hydrate, even if I have to force myself. He's very serious and I take it to heart.

I ask him what the Sherpas are eating for dinner and he says, "Lentils and rice."

"I love lentils and rice. Would it be O.K. if I had some? Is there enough for me to have just a small bite?" Soon the best lentils and rice I've ever had are delivered to my room and I clean my plate.

After dinner, people take turns at the sinks, getting ready for bed. I enjoy listening to their conversations and hearing the laughter. A couple of trekkers are in need of Imodium and the humor turns to childish bathroom jokes. I immediately recognize one of the male voices, but when it begins speaking fluent French, I know I must be wrong.

An unfamiliar couple has to stand outside my door and they're talking to someone at a sink. They're speaking in French and the familiar voice responds. No way! Then the voice laughs and I'm *positive*, it's *Michael.*

After the couple leaves I call out, "Michael?"

He pokes his head in the door with a big smile, "Hey Suzanne, how are you feeling?"

"I'm fine, thank you. Curious, was that *you* speaking French?"

He confirmed it was indeed. He learned the language in the Peace Corps and it's his wife's first language. This guy is multifaceted and I have to admit, *I did not necessarily see that coming.* We've bonded mostly around juvenile humor, so maybe I've pigeon-holed him.

Oh snap, he's probably done the same to me, but I don't have a redeeming talent. I can't speak another language, can't play a musical instrument or sing, and after five years of trying, I still can't juggle.

Mary is a happy distraction when she stops in to say good night. Her motherly instincts are comforting. She asks if I need anything so I tell her, "Just a night-night hug." She snuggles beside me and we chat about the day. She gives me a big hug and says, "Good night, sleep tight, and don't let the bedbugs bite."

"Oh, please Mary, tell me they don't have bed bugs here that bite."

She laughs, "No way! Not at this altitude they don't." She kisses my cheek and I'd bet rupees that I have a red lipstick print on my cheek. I'm grateful for Mary and her red lipstick.

I'd love to be grateful for sleep, because at this point, *it only hurts when I'm conscious.*

A typical meal

Lunch on semi-flat ground

A particulalry impressive suspension bridge

John Richard

Mani Stone pile

Magnificent

Namche

# 14

## September 28, 2012

When I awake, I don't seem to have lingering symptoms from yesterday's crash, but I do have a sore throat, swollen glands, and fluid in my ears. I know my immune system is struggling so I start my Z-pak of antibiotics.

I was diagnosed with Severe Obstructive Sleep Apnea years ago, which means that when I fall asleep, my soft palate collapses and obstructs my airway. I stop breathing for around 20 seconds each time, so my heart has to work over-time all night.

The solution is a CPAP machine that creates a continuous air pressure forcing my airway open. But in all honesty, I've never been highly compliant with the machine. The mask straps get tangled in my hair, head movement shifts the mask and causes air leakage, and the high air flow irritates my throat.

The effects of high altitude on sleep apnea have never crossed my mind, until now. Even so, I'm still unaware that high altitude exacerbates sleep apnea, *and* increases the risk for acute altitude sickness.

When I get to the tearoom for breakfast, I take a seat next to a fellow trekker who's never given me a very friendly vibe. I assume that as we get to know each other better she'll warm up. She says she's into holistic healthcare and quizzes me about my diabetes medication. I tell her I take it at night because it makes me nauseous.

She's terse, "Either you can't read a prescription bottle, or, your doctor is an idiot."

*Dahhaaam!* I'm keenly aware of two truths not everyone's cup of tea, and I don't *wear well* with the rest of them. But what'd I do to her? She introduces honey into her tea, then marries them with her spoon.

I make a mental run through of our previous interactions but, nope, I'm clean. Why is she so *un*Zen?

She continues with an explanation of why the medication *must* be taken in the morning. Her information makes perfect medical sense, and I appreciate it very much. I probably misjudged her.

The conversation ends when Teresa appears with an egg sandwich for me. No one else has been served, so again, I feel guilty. I give her a thankful apology and she brushes me off, "It's just an egg sandwich, eat it before it gets cold." Teresa is becoming one of my favorite all-time people.

I feel so much better after eating. I feel better to the point I want to ask for another egg sandwich, but that's greedy. So instead, I ask someone to pass the bread and peanut butter.

When I see Lhakpa, I explain my need for an ATM, "I planned on going last night but yeah, it didn't work out. I need money for toilet paper and snacks."

He smiles widely and nods in agreement, "Yes. Someone will take you when you're ready."

"Can it be Tenzing? *My* Tenzing? Did you know there are *three* Tenzings in the group?" I start to describe which one is *mine* but Lhakpa stops me, "He's outside," like he knows the right one already. He's got a 33% chance of getting it right, so I head out to the courtyard.

Outside, I study the silhouettes of the Sherpa loading the yak against the bright rising Himalayan sun. I came prepared with sunglasses that can withstand staring contests with *quasars,* so soon enough I'm sure, Tenzing's not here. I turn to go back to the lodge and plow right into Tenzing. He's been standing behind me, watching me, look for him.

He holds out his arm and I scold him, "Ha ha, you're a real hoot. Yeah, you're a *funny* Sherpa man. Better keep your day job." He laughs, "O.K. It's a good day job." How does he know American humor so well? I've never considered the Universal nature of humor, nor thought about it in a cultural or geographic sense. I'm realizing how humor can transcend differences and create immediate connections between people.

I take his arm and although I don't think I need physical assistance, I need a guide for sure. He often shifts sides and arms to accommodate for the constantly changing terrain, always making it easier for me. He's walking beside and around me, in a shielding manner, and it hits me – he's *herding* me.

A group of approaching yak cause my immediate and subtle relocation, to a space between Tenzing and a building. I remember how drawn to Marilyn the yak were yesterday. Do they truly sense suffering? Do they feel sympathy or empathy? Is it something primitive, or is it on a higher plane? Or, is it simply random and coincidental?

If yak do connect to some sort of emotional distress or physical pain, I'd like to know if my current state warrants *yak attention* and here's my chance. I put my hand on Tenzing's shoulder and move forward alone.

He steps aside and I only take a few steps when an oncoming yak turns towards me. I hear Tenzing move and put my hand out, "Please don't shoo it away." This yak has a bead on me with huge bovine eyes that are trying to connect to my soul. Suddenly a porter swats her from behind and she turns back to the herd.

I call to the yak, "No, come back. I didn't catch what you were saying."

It's now clear to me that these animals with their big furry hearts were dying for Marilyn. And at least one of them thought I could use a little one-on-one attention. I love yak.

Tenzing points ahead and motions to the left. I see a sign for an ATM. It's in an entrance to a shop and I recognize it as an artifact from the past. It doesn't run on PASCAL or FORTRON, but it's archaic.

Once a transaction begins, the door is shut from the street, and a curtain is available for privacy. I don't need privacy. I need a financial trekker advisor. I still haven't figured out how to convert rupees and dollars.

My first try fails miserably. I get 40 rupees and an $8 service charge, but I was going for 400 rupees. I focus and re-enter my pin number, *carefully*. On the second try, I score the equivalent of 200 rupees so I'm over half way there. But when I try to access my account again, it's been frozen. I should have given the bank a heads-up before I left the States. Crap. This one's on me.

Tenzing and I walk across the street so I can buy a metal canteen to hold boiled water. It was on the supply list so I need to get one. I've already bought at least three different systems to purify water while trekking, but every one of them has a disclaimer. A fourth can't hurt.

Outside the shop are bins of brightly colored yak wool hats. I joke with the shopkeeper about the different animal heads, including frogs, bears, "angry birds," and horses, as well as hats in solids, and stripes. He has more he wants to show me and quickly brings out two more boxes. After I pick out an even dozen, we go inside for the canteen.

They all look the same to me and so I ask Tenzing for his opinion. He hands me a metal water bottle and I thank him. This is one of our last pit stops and I'm surprised the prices aren't sky high. They have us by the short hairs. Why aren't they gouging? Clearly we're not in the U.S.

As I wait for a total, I hear a loud, irritated, and familiar voice, resonating from the street. It's the *un*Zen caregiver. She sounds disgusted as she talks to her friend waiting on the ATM. "I can't believe these idiot Americans come on a trip like this, completely unprepared. Some don't have Imodium or Diamox, and some don't even know how to take what they do have. We're supposed to be caregivers for them? Whatever."

My face snaps toward Tenzing and his falls to the floor.

Already on edge I snap, "Did you hear her?"

He nods, but doesn't looking up.

I'm pissed off. "Why the hell would she say that?"

I jab my finger at the street and know I'm over-gesturing when Tenzing rests his hand on my forearm. I lower my arm and keep my voice low, but my face is screaming its face off, "I call *bullshit!*"

I must be projecting my thoughts again because I'm certain Tenzing agrees with me. The *un*Zen is a *mean-girl*.

He doesn't say a single word on the way back to the lodge, and I'm trying not to curse again. It's not culturally acceptable and I already let a "hell" and a "bullshit" fly. Walking in silence I wonder why I'm so triggered by her. Did she hit a nerve because *I'm* "an idiot American, unprepared?" There have been hints:

1) I had no idea taking a pill in the morning versus the night could be such a big deal. I realize now why it matters, but I wasn't negligent.

2) I should have trained harder but I give myself a shout out for setting a personal best. Also, altitude doesn't care about training, unless you train at altitude.

3) I'm still fuzzy on the exchange rate and I never thought for a second I'd need more money. I brought a gracious amount from the start, but had to give $200 for Asian Trekking staffs tip. I didn't know about the $200, but I have a debit card. Notifying my bank of foreign travel seemed completely unnecessary, *at the time.*

4) Some things went wrong from the start – the entire trip changed, and Charlie Wittmack got sick, and anxiety started acting

These unexpected changes caused me to feel out of control and panic-stricken; I wanted to back out but I couldn't, or rather, I wouldn't. I believe 100% that I was 100% supposed to come on this trip. But I knew that meant limiting information exposure, carefully and selectively. I trusted Martha knowing that if anyone could help me navigate this adventure, she could. She enlisted her own council and I'd bet the farm they discussed concerns ad nauseam.

By the time we get back to the lodge I've concluded, I'm *not* "an idiot American, unprepared." I'm too winded to talk, and I know I'm gonna have to pick and choose my battles. Unfortunately for this chick, I'm choosing this one. In the meantime, I assure Tenzing I won't say a word until I'm *Buddha chill*.

As luck would have it, the *un*Zen and I are both in the last group, the "Snow Leopards." We have to wait for the first two groups to move on so I have about fifteen minutes which is more than enough time to address her. She's standing in front of the tearoom, next to my backpack, so I head that way.

Tenzing's busy strapping gear on a yak, but he pauses to look at me. He's making sure I'm calm. I feel guilty for getting upset in front of Tenzing and causing him to have to be a Sherpa on an emotional level. I smile at him and bowing, bring my hands together. I mouth, "*Namaste*." I honor the God in him *a lot*.

Bringing his hands together, he tips his head and goes back to work.

I ask to speak with the *un*Zen and we step away from the group. I begin, "I think you'd want to know, I heard what you said about the "idiot Americans being unprepared."

She looks confused.

"When you were outside the ATM earlier, I was inside the shop across the street. I heard what you said."

Her expression doesn't change and she's so slow to respond, I offer another sentence, *verbatim*. She's replaying the tape of herself from earlier, but she's not going to commit because she's not sure what I heard. That doesn't sit well with me.

I feel as if I've been physically pinched and think, "Oh no ma'am! I just told you what I heard. You don't get a pass because *you're not sure*. You're in my wheelhouse now and tracking conversation is second nature to me. If I'm quoting you to your face and you're still not sure, you either don't want to know, or you need a neurologist."

I repeat a few more sentences *verbatim* and her smile dissipates. She's busted but her concession knocks me off balance, "Well, I guess we all need to get checked from time to time."

Basically she's owning her pissy attitude and standing by it. I respect a firm stance and occasional hard-lines, but she's too hard, too soon. After further thought, maybe she's the most rational one of the bunch, and 100% right. Regardless, her karma is none of my business so when I hear, "Let's go Snow Leopards," I'm ready for something completely different.

Today's itinerary reads,

"Our short walk to Khumjung will take us off the beaten path from the tourist path of Namche, to the Sherpa enclave of Khumjung. Khumjung is the former home of Tenzing Norgay, the first man to climb Mount Everest. The village is home to many of the men and women who make their living on Everest and is not typically visited by Western trekkers. In the village, we will have an opportunity to visit a Sherpa school built by Sir Edmund Hillary. If we're lucky, we may also have the opportunity to view the controversial remains of the fabled Himalayan yeti skull."

I recall my own experience *much* differently.

The walk out of Namche is straight up and incredibly difficult for the start of a day. There's no warm up, just an immediate increase in heart rate. It seems it usually takes about 20-30 minutes of walking before my heart and lungs catch up, but today I'm struggling after just a few flights of steps. We're barely out of the village and I'm panting. About twenty yards up I have to stop to catch my breath.

I'm commanding my lungs to expand as the "Rock-Climber Replacement" walks by. He was supposed to take Charlie Wittmack's place, but the only motivation I've heard from him is, "*keep moving.*" I'm not sure if that's Charlie's style too, but if it is, I'd be happy to see *both* of them fall off the side of this mountain.

I warn myself to keep a check on my attitude, but this is so unbelievably hard! Soon enough, I have to pause again, and I bend over to prop myself, hands on knees. A set of shoes parks next to mine and when I trace the pants to the face I see it's Tenzing. I quickly inform him, "No, I don't need anything but *a minute*"—and not a New York minute. I need a **Sherpa minute**."

I ditched my backpack a few steps ago and when I turn to retrieve it, it's over Tenzing's shoulder. As I start back up the trail, his arm now provides a necessary crutch.

We climb for a few more minutes and I feel like there's a knife in my heart. I *have* to stop again. I've gone from "I need a second" to "I need a chair lift" when Dr. Deming arrives and asks, "Are you O.K.?"

I know he's showing compassion, but I don't want attention so I try to divert his. I point in an upward direction, "There's the top. See you on it."

"O.K., take your time." He steps back, remains in my peripheral vision. He's the doctor for the Snow Leopards today so I must be the weakest link. *Damn it.*

After a minute or so I stop panting, and after a few more, I can finally breathe with my mouth closed. Arriving in Namche yesterday was hard as hell. Leaving the place has been a bitch!

Our mid-morning break comes with an unparalleled bonus—our first view of *Mount Everest*. It feels like something out of *The Lord of the Rings*. I'm seeing with my own eyes, in real time, the tallest of the fantasy-like mountains that make up the Himalayas. Every mountain in this chain is spectacular, and at these altitudes, a 360-degree view can be *mind-altering*.

As I sit next to another trekker, I tell him about the note I found two days ago from my daughter Emma, hidden in my luggage in Kathmandu. I've memorized it so when I hand him the note, I read her words aloud and only point in the general direction of each sentence.

"I love you, Mama, and am so proud of you! YOU GOT THIS!!!!" Underneath, she drew a heart and signed her name, "Emma Claire."

When I look at my companion, he has tears in his eyes; I discreetly wipe away my own. The moment is interrupted by Justin, apparently eager to point out the *second* "Guinness World Record" airport we've seen in two days.

He's pointing to a mountain in the distance, "Hey, Suzanne, you know what's up there?"

I think so. "A mountain top?"

"Yeah, but on top of the top."

What I think is, "If God really loves me, an elevator down." What I say is, "I have no idea."

He can't wait to tell me, "That's Syangboche, the world's *highest* airport. We're about to pass right by it!"

Oh, dear Lord, if it's further than I can see, it's further than I can walk.

I call back, "Walking's for wussies and trekking's for people in good shape. *I'm neither* so find us a plane and *I'll* fly us there!"

After successfully flying to the other side of the earth into the World's Most Dangerous Airport, I'm over-confident, approaching cocky. I continue, "I'm thinking of looking into flight school when I get back home…probably gonna get my *wings* and *things*."

Several people laugh, but Dr. Deming isn't one of them. He seems anxious to the point of pained. He's not making eye contact with anything that isn't on top of his boots. He hesitates as he begins, "I'm not sure how to say this, so I'll just say it."

Oh no, this is sad. I bet one of his patients died. I'm so glad I don't know anyone he knows. I feel guilty and wonder, "Is that wrong? Is it wrong to be grateful I can't share in his pain right now? I can't handle any more pain right now."

He continues, "At 6:15 this morning, a flight from Kathmandu to Lukla crashed after takeoff. There were 19 on board and there were no survivors. We're contacting your families to let them know you're safe."

It doesn't take long for me to recognize the person crying is me. For the second time in as many days, my body reacts without my permission. Noises recede, lights dim, and my breath leaves me. My feelings are at war with each other; I feel terrified and numb, hollow and sick. How is it possible to go from such extreme elation to equal amounts of devastation in mere seconds?

In "The Prophet," Kahil Gibran writes "On Joy and Sorrow,"

"They are inseparable. Your joy is your sorrow unmasked. The deeper that sorrow carves into your being, the more joy you can contain. You are suspended like scales between your sorrow and your joy. Only when you are empty are you at standstill and balanced."

I'm nowhere near empty. I'm about to freak out and a red fleece jacket is placed around my shoulders. I remember Tenzing has it.

Leslie appears at my side and I lean into the mother in her. I still can't breathe and I'm inhaling *nothingness*.

My mind is trying to see the whole picture as Janis warns Alice, "Stop crying!"

My biggest fear in life just flipped me the finger and I'm stunned. I work to stay calm telling myself, "It wasn't your plane; you're here and safe, so *breathe*."

Janis doesn't want to be told what to do, "Shut up, I *am* breathing."

The therapist in me knows better, "No, you're not *really* breathing."

Janis hisses, "I *am* breathing, so let it go, Cling-on motherfucker!"

I focus on breathing until I'm struck by what Dr. Deming is saying, "We're getting word to your families to let them know we're O.K."

On the other side of the world, CNN was showing pictures of a plane exactly like ours in the fiery crash, with headlines reading, "Nineteen dead in crash of a plane carrying tourists to Everest staging post." At this very moment, neighbors were knocking on the door to ask Brad if I was O.K. Martha and Mom were calling. Thankfully, Charlie was a step ahead in contacting our families.

Alice is hurting and wants to know, "Why did a plane just like mine crash today? He said 'no survivors.' It could have been my plane. I didn't want to fly to Lukla. I didn't want to get on the plane. It should have been my plane." I know these are irrational thoughts, but they're coming from someone feeling small and helpless.

I take more deep breaths and experience the truth as a knowing, "Yes, I drew attention to myself because of my anxiety and we held hands, prayed, and for a moment hyper-focused on the safety of our plane, that flight, and everyone on it." Take-off was surreal and I felt peace and love, joy, and gratitude.

But my heart is currently twisting in fear and Alice is unreasonable, "Yeah, my flight was magical, but *theirs*, theirs crashed and *everybody* died. It was supposed to have been *my* plane. This disaster was supposed to have to me!"

I know the thoughts are unreasonable. I brought conscious awareness to my flight's safety. But *what if* there *is* some whacked correlation between the two—like the more we focused and prayed, the more we shifted energy. The flight that crashed was too close in time and they got sucked in."

"Who's *they*? Sucked into *what*?"

If this is some kind of cosmic joke, it's *not* funny."

Dr. Deming continues pointing out the different mountains we can see from here, "There's Lhotse, and Ama Dablam, and *that's* Everest." He's pointing at eleven o'clock, the one that's bigger than life.

At any other time, it'd be *magnificent*. But right now, it's nothing but a big dumb pile of rocks. I feel nauseous.

When my brain catches up, I hear Dr. Deming's words repeating in my head, "We're contacting your families to let them know you're safe."

I agree that's a good idea because Martha's gonna hear about this and freak out. She's really going to lose it!

Janis is quick, "Wait a stinkin' second; Martha knows the trip's itinerary inside and out, so she *knows* about Lukla. So, she *knew* about Lukla two days ago, *and* two weeks ago, and never said a word. I hope she does freak out; I hope she *chokes* on freak out!"

Crap, that's not true. I'm sure she struggled over whether to tell me and probably got a few opinions. She knew, if I knew about Lukla, I wouldn't go. And I wouldn't have.

But wait a tic. That means Brad also knew about Lukla…and so did Phil, and so did Emma. Now I know why Emma laughed at me in the car on the way to the airport when I said, "Martha's told me everything I need to know."

Aww, come on y'all!

I feel far away, hurting and hollow at the same time, and inexplicably lonely.

Leaving Namche

With Richard Deming and Mt. Everest

We were just told about the plane crash

Andy on the trek to Khumjung

# 15

## This is Nothing Like the Itinerary
*(Trek to Khumjung—12,400 ft.)*

The rest of the morning my mind is a million miles away. As we arrive at today's destination and descend the steps into the village of Khumjung, excited children greet us. They're wearing uniforms of navy pants and sweater, a white shirt, and a navy striped tie. The uniforms seem oddly formal, yet exactly proper. I look at these children and feel a little safer.

The entire village gathers as Dr. Deming makes a short presentation to the school children and gives them several bags of school supplies and athletic equipment.

I've gagged so many times my sides hurt, and I took a ***big*** psychological hit this morning. As soon as possible, I head to the lodge. I'm so tired I skip the field trip to see a Yeti Skull and visit Ang Lhakpa's home for tea and cookies. I'm bummed; I want to see a freakin' yeti skull and I really want cookies at Ang Lhakpa's house.

The acronym HALT flashes and I know I'm all of them—too hungry, too angry, too lonely, and too tired. Alice wants to cry so Janis stands emotional guard.

My mind and body are on high alert so resting is difficult and sleep is impossible. I'm used to operating with little sleep, but this level of fatigue is getting to me.

I give up and sit on my bed to make a prayer flag from borrowed materials. On a yellow square of fabric, I use green and red sharpies. I draw a plane with a big sun and write,

"Kathmandu to Lukla (heart symbol) September 28, 2012

Dear God, Thank you for embracing these souls. I pray you grant peace to all that loved them. Amen."

This evening after dinner Bikal tells me that Charlie Wittmack wants to talk to me when I get back to my room. It's around eight in the morning in Charlotte and while everyone there is beginning their day, I'm grateful mine is over. As soon as I hear his voice, I have to know, "Oh, Charlie, did you hear?"

He's calm. "Yes, I heard."

I'm not as calm. "Everyone died! No survivors Charlie."

It feels like nitpicking when he says, "But it didn't have anything to do with *Lukla*. The plane crashed in *Kathmandu*, 500 yards after taking off. It was a bird strike."

I mumble, "A *bird* strike?"

"Yes, but actually it was a *buzzard*, and a *random* thing that could happen anywhere. "

I'm *incredulous*, "It was a random buzzard?"

He emphasizes the point, "Yes, but in Kathmandu, **not** Lukla."

"Who was on the plane Charlie?"

"Trekkers, mostly British, a few Chinese, and the Nepali crew."

I whisper, "Two pilots and the lady that brings the cotton and the candy?"

He whispers back, "Yeah."

I beg myself not to cry and my response is almost inaudible, "A plane like *ours*?" He seems hesitant to answer more questions and I'm done asking them.

I tell him about my physical crash last night and the struggle leaving Namche this morning. I insist I'm feeling better and he tells me, "Don't worry, many times the people that crash early end up the strongest. Just because you're having a hard time now doesn't mean it'll get worse, or that you can't make it. You're getting it out of the way early."

He asks me questions for his daily updates and I admit, "I'm probably the *worst* person to get rational or helpful information at this point."

"I know the plane crash hit you hard, but this real world shit happens all the time. Just stay calm."

I know he's trying to be supportive and helpful but unfortunately, he just used a *huge* trigger phrase, "Calm down."

Janis instantly rants in my head, "Don't tell me to stay calm. I *am* calm. I'm the essence of calm while you're at (10 East Blvd. You're the essence of warm, rested, and unchafed, replete with clean water and unlimited toilet paper."

I'm calm when I speak, "Look, Charlie, I don't need you to calm me down. I am calm, dude. What I need you to do is *pray for me.* Maybe light a candle when you pass my door."

He stays serious, "Suzanne, I know you can do it. I'm disappointed I'm not there to help you. But *you can definitely* do this."

I need to believe him so I choose to buy-in: hook, line and sinker. But there'd better be a good explanation or lesson in here somewhere; I don't feel safe. Extreme experiences create extreme insights, so I can't imagine the lessons from this one. Although this one seems to be too big to be *just one* lesson.

Janis rales, "It was *a random buzzard.* Not even a Kamikaze or Special Forces buzzard …just some random aloof motherfucker flying around with its thumb up its ass, so it flies into a plane's engine. A SMALL plane, taking up almost no space, *then* **BAM***!* Lives *gone*: fathers and sons, *gone*. Husbands, *gone*. And the one female flight attendant that passed out candy and cotton …*gone. ALL GONE!*"

Ruth enters and tries to console me because it's obvious, I'm *not* in a good headspace.

A knock at the door is followed by Dr. Deming on the other side, "Suzanne? May I come in?"

I wonder why he's here. The last time I saw him, he was in a state of emergency. He'd pushed past me to get into the toilet, apologizing, "Excuse me please …pardon me …*emergency* …" I couldn't hold my laugh or get out of his way fast enough.

I invite him in and after pleasantries, he asks to speak with me in private. I assure him that if the privacy is for *my* benefit, Ruth can stay.

He tells me sympathetically, "I understand you've struggled physically yesterday *and* today. I want you to know that the staff and I have a *plan B,* if you need it. There are others that may stay here in Khumjung too. A Sherpa will take you on incredible day trips, but less strenuous. We'll all meet back in Lukla."

What *he said* was, "You don't need to worry or pressure yourself, and you'll have a fantastic experience no matter what."

What I *heard* was, "You're not cutting it, you're not gonna cut it, so *we're cutting you.*"

He tells me to sleep on it and wishes Ruth and me a good night.

Wow thanks. *Don't count on me.*

Ruth continues packing while I vent. "I can't believe this crap. I'm getting axed with people that need to call it quits, people that *want* to call it quits. Marilyn told me at dinner she wants stay here, but Kim wants to go on. She's determined to support Kim, so she's moving on too and I don't blame her."

I haven't held the line up for one second, but *I'm* a special needs case? I know I've struggled but I don't want to stay here – no offense to *here*, because *here* is amazing. I want to go with the group, but he's offering ...no he's *encouraging* me, to call it quits."

I wish I could get word to Charlie because he'd tell Deming I'm up to it. He'd tell him to believe in me and that'd be the end of it. I know Dr. Deming is just being thoughtful, but I'm so spent, his graciousness is the last straw.

This altitude stuff is relentless and I've been fighting a sore throat, fluid in my ears, and swollen glands, since Namche. Now I have to add emotional pain of rejection and inadequacy.

My chest tightens as I sense my mother reminding me, "Don't be a burden."

I hear my brother's disdain, "You're gross and nobody wants you here anyway."

My father's nonverbal message seems almost calming at this point, "You're so unimportant you're *invisible*." I'd sure like to be invisible right now.

When I awake I feel stronger in every way. But being an extremely sensitive person, I'm still a little butt-hurt, so when I go to breakfast, I'm on guard. I don't want to see Dr. Deming and this group is big enough that with minimal effort, I should be able to avoid him. I enter the tearoom and a short scan lands me in eye contact – son of a bitch; Deming is harder to avoid than a Kathmandu temple monkey.

But he's on the other side of the room so maybe I can escape. Does he know I need glasses? How good is *his* vision? Maybe if I didn't see him, he didn't see me.

His head disappears for a second and I charge into the densest part of the crowd. When I look up again, he's not only closer, *he's waving*. I switch to offense and make a beeline to him.

My forced smile is met with his real one, plus a hug, and a genuine inquiry, "How are you feeling today?"

I'm not sure what his angle is yet, so it's best if I drive, "Look, I know I've struggled, but I've suffered in silence, I do self-care, and I'm not a danger to myself or others. That has to count for something. I'm telling you …I've got this! So unless something changes, *you can't kick me off the island!*"

I spin to leave and he calls my name. I suspect that whole "…you can't kick me off the island" thing was too hard.

I turn and see him standing, very Jesus-like, with arms open, patient and loving. I return for the reassuring embrace and hear the smile in his voice, "That's exactly what I think too."

Trek to Khumjung

Andy

Entering Khumjung - I'm far Right

Dr. D addressing older students of The Hillary School

Leslie with Hillary School Students

This morning's view

Amazing watercolor of Student by Kristin Katich Sumbot - 2013

# 16

## No MONKeying Around
*(Trek to Tengboche–12,664 ft.)*

The climb to Tengboche is arduous. The trail traverses high along the mountainside above the timberline. The weather is perfect and the panoramic views of the Mountains are magical—Everest, Nuptse, Lhotse, and my favorite, Ama Dablam. I have to compartmentalize them into sections, then weave them back together to create one view. The ability to recall this panorama will only be limited by my ability to absorb it in the here and now.

Ama Dablam is 22,500 ft. high and means "Mother's necklace." The long ridges on each side of the peak appear as the arms of a mother protecting her child. Her shawl is made of the snow and I think it's the most beautiful of all these glorious mountains. At this altitude we're close to the sun, so even with cool temperatures it's hot and I'm sweating.

We're all trying to stay hydrated, which comes with a preference for salty foods. Dr. Deming says he could go for a salty snack and declines several offers of sweets, repeating the same thing each time, "No thank you, I want something salty." When more snacks are offered and declined he repeats, "No, I want *salty*, salty like a *salt lick*."

I groan, "*Alright already*, we get it, *salty. I'm sweaty*, you can *lick me* if you'll move on." I'm immediately struck by the inappropriateness of both my tone and statement and I hear Michael cracking up. Dr. Charlie exclaims, "I'd love to be in therapy with you!"

I spout back, "*Please.* You couldn't handle being in therapy with me."

"O.K. you're probably right. But I'd make it through at least three sessions with you."

"You might make it through the first one, but you'd cry and never come back."

He laughs hard, "That's sounds more likely."

Dr. Deming joins in, *positive* he could make it through therapy with me. I agree but look at Dr. Charlie and shake my head *no*. I whisper to the side, "It'd be like shooting fish in a barrel. *I'm not gonna do that.*"

Later while walking with Reverend Richard, he tells me his cancer isn't *curable*, just temporarily treatable. I don't understand temporarily treatable – either you have it or you don't, so to speak …but no matter what, I can't cry. Not front of the man with the *temporarily treatable* cancer; *I have no right*.

Three weeks after my last round of chemotherapy, I felt worse than ever. I knew my surgical sites were clear, but my fever was high. When I called the oncologist's office, I was told it wasn't chemo-related. Brad took me to my primary doctor, who sent me straight to the emergency room.

When we got to the ER, I was put in a sealed room. The nurse suggested to the Doctor that the issue may be with my power port. The doctor thought pneumonia and ordered chest scans. When the x-rays came back clear, I was discharged.

My temperature escalated and the next day I felt worse. I can always tell when I have a fever because I cry for no reason. At this point I couldn't stop crying so I started praying, "I've already called the oncologist, I've seen my primary doctor, *and* I've gone to the ER. I don't know what else to do and I'm getting worse. *Please God, show me what else to do.*"

I got out of bed to get tissues and take a shower to cool down. When I passed the mirror I saw bright neon blue veins all across the left side of my chest. The thought was crystal clear, "Call the surgeon."

I called Dr. Turks office and when I described my symptoms, the nurse didn't hesitate, "It sounds like you have a blood clot in your neck, probably from the power port."

I was paralyzed for a second before I could ask, "The kind that breaks off and goes to your brain, and *kills you*, kind of blood clot?"

She paused, and paused, and paused, then said, "Could you please hold?"

The hold button prompted elevator music. *What a Wonderful World* began mid-song and I lost myself in a geyser of tears. I was depleted and needed a break. I sobbed into the receiver, "I want my Mommy!"

It never occurred to me that some people with cancer run out of options. I feel like a wimp but I'll be strong for Reverend

Richard. As we walk, his humor keeps sadness at bay. What a *fantastic* attitude! He inspires me enough to confide in him a dark realization, "The chances of someone in this group dying from something other than cancer, is a lot less than normal."

He chuckles at my awareness, "Yeah, for sure, cancer survivors are a slippery demographic."

I burst out laughing in appreciation. He hasn't met a level of suffering so cruel that could dampen his sense of humor. He's **always** *Buddha Chill!*

Late in the morning, the clouds arrive with us in the tiny village of Tengboche, the spiritual center of Sherpa Buddhism in the Khumbu valley. A spiritual hub of any kind is a big deal to me. I've studied religions of the East, but Nepal has given me permission to expand my spirituality exponentially.

Our lodging is primitive with interior wall-to-wall ply board, including the ceilings and floors. The second story bathroom is a hole in the floor with a bucket for waste paper. I can't imagine how the septic system works; as the smell worsens, it's clear that the septic system *doesn't work*.

After lunch, we go to *the* monastery to observe the monks' prayer service. In the courtyard, several signs in multiple languages, *plainly* state, **No Photographs Allowed**. Some signs translate into hieroglyphics so you'd have to be an idiot or an asshole, *not* to get the message.

We enter the main room and sit in three rows against a sidewall. The main area is for the monks, and hey, it's for Lhakpa too. I'd heard he's a devout Buddhist, but he must be super special. He's meditating *with* the monks.

All the spectators are with our A+BC group except for a few sitting in the back corner. Soon after the service begins, I hear a camera click and spin around. It's an outsider and he's taking pictures! How did he miss all the signs? When I stare at him he tucks his camera between his legs and looks away from me. Holy cow, he *knows* he's wrong.

The head monk looks for the camera but doesn't turn his head far enough, so his stare falls on me. I'm clearly not taking pictures but his look is upsetting. His jaws clenched, and I swear, he's *flaring a nostril*. It's obvious he's no longer in a peaceful, meditative state. He's disappointed and irritated, and Alice is instantly triggered. My chest tightens and I try to figure out how to let him know it's not me, *I'm not the bad one.*

He returns to meditating but the clicking resumes, and my heart stops. Janis goes on alert and I cork screw to see who dares; but he's closed his eyes as if in prayer. When I turn back to the monk I'm horrified because he's looking at me *again*. I lock eyes with him and jerk my head in dramatic fashion to the perp. I contort my face into what I hope reads unmitigated disgust and point my swollen pointer finger at the blasphemer.

That's when I realize *why* he's looking at me. His view is obstructed, and I'm the last person in his field of vision. Maybe he thinks I know the guy and can get word to him.

What if he thinks it's a member of Lhakpa's group? Lhakpa's sitting at the very back of the room with his eyes closed, and the chanting and occasional gong strikes easily obscure the camera noise. I think Lhakpa would stop the guy himself if he knew.

Janis makes an executive decision, "The monk is a righteous and holy dude and if he goes off, it'll ding his karma. I'll take the karmic hit right after I drag the prick out by the camera strap around his neck." I strain my neck to look for the shortest route to get to him, but unfortunately, he's moated by people and walls. Janis has the solution. "It's time for everybody to *make a hole*. I'm going in."

I unfold my legs and turn, but before I can whisper-shout the order, Ruth taps my arm. She mouths, "I need to go." Even in this dim lighting I can tell her face is an unnatural shade of pale. She whispers, "I need to go right now."

I help her up and grab our backpacks, but on the way out, I stare at the sinner. His head's bowed as if in prayer, and I hope he feels guilty as hell. Then I notice the light from his camera's LCD screen reflecting off the wall. He doesn't give a rat's ass, he's reviewing his work! My knee-jerk reaction is thwarted as soon as sunlight breaks through the room. I know Ruth's reached the lobby and I'm forced to abandon my **public-service act** of taking out the trash.

We're still putting our shoes on when the rest of the group shows up. Turns out, the monk ended the service early because of the photographing. I can't believe the disrespect. What makes someone feel so immune to the rules?

I want this guy to explain to me, right to my face, why he's entitled to do whatever the hell he wants. Then I want to make him cry for doing it to MONKS!

I'm still worked up so I wonder, "How do monks calm themselves? Will this one take a shot of whiskey, or have a glass of wine? Do monks smoke *weed*?"

He's a chill guy but I bet he gets super tired of under-evolved tourist turds. He probably meditates on creative ways for them to die, including a good old-fashioned yak stampeding.

Note to self – "*Stop projecting your thoughts and feelings onto others.*"

Back in the room, Ruth hurls herself onto her bed, and then hurls her lunch into the bedside bucket. Man she's really sick. That totally explains her hue. She throws up and up and up, so the garbage can fills quickly. The smell is awful so I open the door to the lobby area where Father Frank is preparing for evening Mass.

I catch Dr. Deming's eye and while he attends to Ruth, I head to the bathroom to empty the pail. I sneak quickly past Father Frank in his long white robe and purple sash. One step into the bathroom stops me dead in my tracks. It's like entering a *yak poo sauna;* it's hot and smells repulsive. I start to pour the pail into the hole and when it collides with what's already inside, it makes a disgusting noise, and I gag so hard. I make a run for the door but have to inhale and gag again, this time harder and longer. If it happens again, it's gonna get ugly.

One last inhale and I'm in the hall, but not out of danger. As I bolt past Father Frank I'm grateful for a single distracting thought, "How is that robe not wrinkled?" By the time I'm back in the room my eyes are beyond watering, they're tiny geysers. Dr. Deming thinks something's wrong but I assuage his concern, "No, no, it's the smells…the vomit (I mouth the words)…*the poo*."

He starts to laugh and I whisper-chide, "It's not funny! I almost threw up…*on throw up!*"

Laughing harder he grabs his sides.

I point to the Catholic Mass on the other side of the plywood and whisper loudly, "You're not being a good Catholic, and you're *not* role-modeling *compassion!*" He's caught off guard, swallows wrong, chokes a little.

I shake my head vigorously while wagging an equally riled-up finger at him, "Good enough on you. My work here is done." I do appreciate his sense of humor.

I walk to the window and look out. My gaze is immediately drawn below where I see Mary. She's washing Ruth's bucket as clouds begin to settle around her feet. Her short dark hair resists moisture from the misting rain, creating a helmet of glistening water-beads.

I smile when I notice, Mary's wearing fresh lipstick.

Trek to Tengboche - fearless yak

Tengboche

Dr. Deming receiving a blessing

A Buddhist Priest

Inside the Monestary

# 17

## Ala Freakin Bama

*(Trek to Dingboche—14,468 ft.)*

Today's morning rituals are held in front of the monastery. Judith, our *Peaceful Angel* starts our day with Qigong movements that allow us to gently twist and turn as we enjoy the views all around us. Enormous mountains surround the tiny village, causing everything in it to appear shrunken. The white snow-capped peaks are stark against the blue of the sky.

By mid-morning, everything about this day is perfect. I've been talking with people in the "Yak" group, Michael in particular. We haven't been in the same group yet, so we give each other visual high fives when we hear our names called together. We've connected through humor, so we've definitely connected.

As we trek to Dingboche, I listen to different songs from my Hello Kitty MP3 player, often sharing the earbuds. Michael likes Janis Joplin's *Mercedes Benz* and wants to sing it out loud, but he doesn't know the words *or tune*. He keeps saying, "Go ahead and start us up again Suzanne, just one more time." But when he hears the song by Trace Adkins, *Ala Freakin Bama* and he's hooked. He listens to it over and over, blasting the chorus, "Tell me what's it to ya? I'm from Ala freakin Bama!"

Hello Kitty gets passed around and I hear half a dozen people, several with Nepalese accents, sing "I'm from Ala freakin Bama!" These are good people, and this is a good time. I have no reason to be homesick, I'm with family.

Dr. Deming appears out of nowhere. He can't wait to get in on the whole *Ala Freakin Bama* thing. He's always in the right place at the right time, so after he puts in the ear buds, he begins dancing up the trail.

It's worth noting that this particular stretch is *steeply* inclined and above 14,000 ft. to begin with!

Michael and I pause when we hear him in the distance, "I'm from Ala freakin Bama, Bama!" *Everybody* cracks up. He's obviously much further up the trail than the rest of us.

Soon he reappears, dancing a circle around us, "She wore a pink Bama do-rag, smackin' on juicy fruit." He yells at me, "This is my new favorite song!"

The next sighting has him about ten yards behind us, heel-clicking his way back. By this time he's struggling and winded, but still giving it his all, "Baby, open up a can of Ala freakin Bama, hey!" Man, he really digs this song *a lot*.

I have to stop walking because now he's bent over in front of me, hands on knees, gasping, "I'm …not …a quitter, but how long …is …this song? Does it …*ever* end?"

I give it to him straight, "It's as long as you want it to be darlin.' It's on replay!"

Everyone reacts. We've all enjoyed his spunk, determination, confusion, decline into pain, perseverance and last-ditch plea.

The expression on his face as he peels the ear buds out is hysterical. He can't believe what he just put himself through, but he knows there's no one else to blame, he did this to himself. He gently scrunches Hello Kitty together and tosses it in my general direction. I catch the device and know I can't hold myself much longer.

Make no mistake, it's a group moment, but Michael and I are the worst. He's gasping for air and I'm in the middle of a full-on roar. I'm acutely aware our laughter has been at this dear man's expense and I want to stop, but I can't. Remember, I have ILS, so don't judge me.

But worse than laughing at him is the fact I goad him, "Are you *sure* you're done? I've got more batteries."

Dr. Deming shakes his head and waves me off.

"I'm impressed by your sportsmanship!"

He seems pretty proud of himself too, and retells the story at lunch. A few people ask to hear the song, so I borrow Teresa's speaker. By the end, everyone's singing "Ala freakin Bama, Bama!"

Michael wants to share a few other songs we've learned, and I try hard to find them. Understand, the screen for the Hello Kitty MP3 is about 1 by 2 inches, poorly lit, and I've needed glasses for *years*. Also, we're under the Himalayan sun. I have to put my coat over my head to create shade to read the screen. When I think I've found Monty Python's *Always Look on the Bright Side of Life*, I hit play.

Monty Python blasts through the speaker, but it's the wrong song. Instead, they're singing, "Sit on my face and tell me that you love me. I'll sit on your face and tell you I love you too."

"No, no, no, that's dirty!" I panic and rip half my hair out trying to get my coat off.

Monty Python continues, "I love to hear you moralize when I'm between your thighs. You blow me away!"

I yell as loudly as I can, "No, don't listen! La la, *cover your ears!*"

A quick glance at Hello Kitty reminds me that changing the volume requires going through four screens, none of which I can see. I decide to turn the volume off, but the speaker doesn't have a volume button.

Monty Python crescendos, "Life can be fine if we both 69…"

Now I give one long scream, "Noooooooo!!!!!" I rip out the cord.

Many aren't sure if they really heard a song about sitting on someone's face, but from those that know, the uproar is tremendous. Michael is the loudest until Dr. Deming proclaims, "Oh no! Susannah Bama!"

Michael yells, "Way to go, *Ala freakin Bama*!" My nickname Bama is born.

I feel strongly the doctor and I are now even, and I'm equally certain, I now owe Michael one.

Morning rituals - Monestary in Tengboche

Leaving Tengboche toward a cloud covered Everest

A face down Leslie and I waiting for the lunch crowd.

I have the speaker in my hand and things are about to go wrong.

With Michael before the fallout

# 18

## Blessed Be My Tie-Dyed Underwear
### *(and Mingma Sherpa too)*

After lunch, the trek to Dingboche is mostly uphill where finally, it's cold. We're staying at The Paradise Lodge, owned by female Everest climber, Mingma Sherpa. She's a member of the all-women Nepali expedition in 2006 and deserves great respect and admiration for many her contributions to her community. We get to stay at a real heroine's lodge, for two consecutive nights. Talk about a win-win! Repacking the duffle bag every morning is time-consuming, renegotiating the crampons and ice pick into alliances with all the other stupid things in it is a pain in the ass.

But Ruth doesn't complain about anything, much less packing. She can unpack and repack before I can get my backpack off. I try to follow her efficiency from my bed.

Tomorrow, we'll summit the 16,500 ft. Nangkar Tshang, but first things first. I have to do laundry because I'm critically low on clean underwear. A large and clearly printed sign reads, "No laundry in shower."

But I'm almost out of my clean, moisture wicking, white boxers. I rationalize, "I'll just wash one specific section of each pair, and I won't put conditioner on my hair."

I still feel guilty, but I'm trying to create balance, and, *clean underwear.*

Maybe I'll be considered a criminal if they find out I compromised their *suggestion*. Wait a tic. Is this how the camera tourist in the monastery rationalized taking pictures? I am most certainly *not* like him!

My conscience clucks its tongue loudly and warns, "Slippery slope Suzanne. Slippery slope."

Once back in the room, I have clean-*ish* underwear, but they're wet so I have to find somewhere to hang it. I think about outside the window, but I'm not sure I could crawl back in. Ruth is ready to go to dinner so I don't have time for a test run.

Then I have a brilliant idea. The room next to ours is vacant, so I can hang them in there, discreetly out of the way. I impress myself with a solution for the clothesline…two miniature strands of prayer flags given to me by a shopkeeper in Namche Bazar. I tie them together and drape the underwear over them.

As soon as I get back to our room and announce my success, the power goes out. It's been blinking off and on which isn't unusual, but now it's pitch black. Thankfully, Ruth's wearing her headlamp. I ask her to shine it around my area so I can find mine. It has to be close by because I had it on mere *minutes* ago.

She moves her head back and forth like a lighthouse on meth. It's way too quick for me to focus so I suggest, "Yes, just like that, but a ton slower."

She's getting impatient because she doesn't want to be late for dinner. She is always ready and prepared and on time. Being saddled with a struggling slacker *has got to be* frustrating. As she backs into the hallway, the light from her headlamp becomes dimmer and dimmer, until it's useless.

I'm sarcastic. "Good grief, you may as well go on to the tearoom."

Before I can tell her I'm kidding, footsteps fade. Before I can speak the thought "Oh my god, *no* not really," the footsteps fade. I don't call out because I'm positive she's making a joke.

I reach behind me to feel my bed and find a spot to sit while I wait for the joke to play out. After a long silence, I call "Ruth?" The silence is deafening, so I repeat louder, "Ruth?" Still nothing.

She's really gone. She *really* left me in total darkness! I can't see my hand in front of my face.

Just as I get irritated, I hear footsteps; the glow of a headlamp offers faint light from the end of the hallway. I think, "Oh, Suzanne, be ashamed of yourself."

The light gets closer but disappears. I hear keys opening the door across the hall and I call out, "Hello?"

After a pause, the dim light enters my room and a headlamp answers, "Yes? Hello?" It's Lhakpa, and while I can't see his face, his tone wants to know why I'm sitting here alone, *in the dark*.

I ramble off an incoherent excuse and when I find my headlamp under my bed I thank him. I also head out, stomp down the hall, around the next corner, down another hall, around *another* corner, and finally into the lodge that leads to the tearoom. I walk in looking for Ruth and trouble.

When I see her, I pitch our room key down and blurt, "Jesus, Root! Seriously?"

Why the hell did I just call her Root? I feel badly when she winces and looks confused. Guilt steps up but begs the question, "Did you hear me say to wait?"

"No, I didn't hear you say anything."

I should have realized it was her hearing since I've been pouring hydrogen peroxide in her ear every night. I sincerely apologize, "Sorry Root. Here's our room key. I'm going outside in the cold to shame myself alone."

After dinner, I notice the door to the room in which I hung my underwear is shut *and locked*. Ruth and I talk about what to do when I hear the door being unlocked. I'm relieved. "Ruth, I'll just go get my underwear from whoever moved in and apologize for any inconvenience."

"Yeah," she says, "that's a better idea than you hanging your underwear in there."

"Gee, Hon, I wish you'd said that *before* I McGyvered a clothesline and *defi*led prayer flags."

I run to the scene of the crime and Mingma is standing in the middle of the room, arms in the air, assessing the situation. Underwear is drying over the holy flags of her mother country.

But they look different and when I realize why I want to die. Every pair is uniquely tie-dyed the colors of Tibetan prayer flags: red, green, blue, and yellow.

I've gotta decide right now whether or not underwear is worth *Locked Up Abroad*. Sacred Religious Blasphemy probably carries a lengthy sentence, and Mingma doesn't look happy. I could lie my way out of the room because the underwear are men's boxers. I could pretend to be upset with her and be all like, "Nooooo! Who would have done this terrible thing? Do you have any suspects? May I clear the crime scene for you?"

Oh sweet Lord! Who am I kidding? I won't consciously hurt anyone, and I'll travel twice as far to avoid hurting an animal. And I'm positive... I *cannot* go a week without clean underwear.

I throw myself on the sword and blurt, "Oh, Mingma! I know how this must look, I'm so sorry! I didn't mean to be disrespectful *I swear*! I didn't think it through; *please* forgive me."

She starts laughing and I take it as a sign; she's not too upset.

I open my arms and suggest, "Let's hug it out and put this whole *soiled* thing behind us."

She hugs me back as I lean in and begin ripping the "clothesline" down. As my once white underwear propels in multiple directions, I snag a pair mid-flight. In my hand is a display of all the colors of earth's elements.

Mingma hides her smile behind her hand.

Dr. Deming and Mingma Sherpa - Paradise Lodge

Dingboche

Judith and Dr. D

Morning rituals

# 19

# The One They Call Bama is Lost Again
*(Summit of Nangkar Tshang—15,806 ft.)*

The next morning we start climbing the 15,000 ft. high mountain, Nangkar Tshang. The clouds in Nepal can be sneaky and have minds of their own. They appear, descend, disappear, reappear, ascend or not, and available combinations. When the sun peeks through I can see forever, but when it's hidden I can't see my own shoes.

I've been walking with Jeff for the past half hour. I thought he was funny when he introduced himself at Fire and Ice Pizza the first night in Kathmandu. "Some people call me Jeff, but most know me as Dr. Feel Good." His smile lit his face so he was on my radar – a happy person with a good sense of humor.

I remember how he walked with Leslie, Kristin, and me, as we searched for beads in Kathmandu. He switched seats with Father Frank on the flight to Lukla, and was in that life-saving prayer circle. He helped me and many others down wet, slippery stones, from Lukla to Phakding. I appreciate, respect, and like Jeff very much.

As we approach the summit I notice a lot of people are getting their asses kicked, so I feel better. Wait, No! What? I just mean that I I'm fifty yards up the mountain from Jeff when I turn around to catch my breath and let him catch up. He's pausing too, followed patiently by a Sherpa.

What I see snags my breath. The crevasses and curves paint masterpieces. The view gets closer to 180 degrees the higher we ascend. On my left is the village, although it's minuscule at this point. Mountain ranges extend in every direction for further than the eyes can track. These mountains aren't normal, nor do they follow the rules for normal mountains. *Normal* mountains don't grow higher than clouds. But when I look at them relative to each other, they form a reasonable average.

I simultaneously watch, sense, smell, and hear this place, and start crying. In this moment, I feel *complete* peace and happiness. I am in the present and soaking up every molecule. Someone higher up the mountain yells down to me, "Bama, are you crying?"

"Yeah, it's just so beautiful."

John Richard points his camera at me, "What are you thinking right now?"

I have to take a deep breath, "Gratitude. I feel so much gratitude and so much love. I just wanna mash everybody. *Mash*, there's you a southern term."

Because the clouds have temporarily surrendered, I can see the top of Nangkar Tshang and several *Stupas* (Sanskrit for pile of rocks meant for meditation) connected by strands of prayer flags. The stupas are formed as travelers pass and add a stone, and say a prayer.

Clearly, this mountain wants to keep its summit challenging, so within seconds the clouds squeeze back in.

Dr. Leah and I have been walking together and I discover my suspicion was right; she does have a wicked good sense of humor. At some point I respond to her with, "That's what she said." She laughs but I want to be sure I didn't offend her. "I'm sorry. That was inappropriate."

She deadpans, "That's what she said."

At least half the group is already descending and a caregiver passes and says, "Ala *freakin'* Bama, somebody kissed your *freakin'* face."

I remember I have a big red lip kiss on my cheek, "Yeah, it was Mary – for luck."

The reply is deadpan, "Well it's working. You're almost there."

I've tripped and stumbled for a couple of hours and when I finally see Dr. Deming standing at the summit, he greets me with applause, "Good job Suzanne."

"Thank you, sir."

The top of the mountain is a small surface about the size of a trampoline, so only a handful of people can be on top at once. Because the clouds are temporarily obscuring all views, I Chevy Chase it – three head bobs – and I head back down.

Compared to up, down is a breeze but the clouds still play hide and seek. I'm worried about Ruth even though she's in better shape than 95% of us. She didn't bring a prosthetic arm because it gets in the way of using her remaining limb. Some parts of the summit require crawling over large rocks, so the descent is especially tricky. When the clouds blanket the ground, it's flat-out dangerous.

Leah and I got separated so I've been walking alone listening to music, and as Hello Kitty enhances the earth's sensory appeal, I blissfully follow a group of red fleece jackets. When a village appears, I become uneasy. The names on the rooftops are different. And hey, how did they build that fence in the last few hours?

This is completely wrong. Before I can get alarmed, I hear whistling and spin around. A Sherpa frantically waves his arms from atop the nearest ridge. He's pointing me in the opposite direction. I look back and all the red fleece jackets have disappeared.

Son of a gun, I've been following the wrong group.

I hold a thumb up to let him know I understand, and then the other one to thank him. I wonder how he knew I was astray, or did we both just get lucky.

I have to make up for lost time so I walk with purpose. When I get to the top of the next ridge and look down, I'm confused. I don't recognize anything and at least a half an hour has gone by. Telling time by the position of the sun has become a new hobby. It's well past noon for sure, probably closer to one, and I'm tired and hungry.

In the valley directly below sits a camp of orange tents; men in dark uniforms diligently work. The whole vibe is serious and shakes me out of tired, hungry and *hugely* irritated at myself. I move to a high level of *on-guard.*

I've been watching the scene below for several minutes when my lower back gets my attention. It's super tight so without a second thought, I bend over to stretch-out my hamstrings. The weight in my backpack shifts downward, towards my head. I sense sudden forward motion and comprehend Road Runner fast, according to the laws of gravity, I won't stop until I split the campfire.

I buckle my knees while jerking my body backwards. It's an ugly win but I drop like a rock and end all forward motion. I land hard on my butt and berate myself, "What a total dumbass. Of all the stupid things you could do, *I did not see this one coming!*"

My heart's racing because according to the laws of physics, I should have tipped over face-first. What if the camp is Nepal's *Locked Up Abroad* prison site? Why am I so stuck on that show?

I sit hidden behind a large rock, heart still pounding from the most recent stupid move I've made. In addition to fart-startled, I'm tired, hungry, and lost. I recognize this as a big HALT moment.

I mimic Dr. Deming. "You can do it, Susannah Bama, can't you? You can do just one more step. You can climb one of the highest mountains in the world and get lost twice, and probably *die* on the way down, *can't you?*"

Of course I can. *I can do the hell out of dumbass.*

I have to get down the mountain to *any*where, but I can't see what's over the next ridge and I don't know the name of our lodge. But surely everybody in the village knows where Mingma lives.

Hello Kitty is full of static and suddenly stops working. The single AAA battery has died and I don't have a spare in my backpack. I don't mind because it's in the middle of a Steve Martin routine that I know by heart … the one where he has to get handcuffs for his cat, "and he's gotta get 'em fast."

I'll have to face the music without music.

I decide the safest route starts in the direction from which I've come. I stand up and put my backpack on, then see the same Sherpa bolt over the ridge right behind me. We both have mirroring reactions of relief. He runs down and grabs my arm and I accuse him, "You thought you lost me again, didn't you? You thought you lost me *twice*. Well you did! You did lose me *twice*, so *stop* losing me! And hey, "Radar?" Thanks for *finding* me twice too."

He's clapping and as I reach out to hug him, I notice the color has returned to his face. He's young and I'm sure he doesn't want a bad mark stamped on his permanent record: "Lost a trekker in 2012."

We walk the rest of the way down with my new friend Radar, no more than two feet from my side. I try to assure him, "Relax. I wasn't playing hide and seek, and I'm most certainly not a flight risk." He nods in understanding, but he stays attached to my hip.

I have to know so I ask, "How did you know I was lost, again? How'd you find me, *again*?"

Do Sherpa have ESP, or is it something along the lines of Secret Service? I haven't seen earpieces. I imagine what their radio chatter would sound like: "The one they call lazy is still sitting at the bridge. The one they call Bama is lost, *again*. Who's on her? Nearest eye locate and escort squirrel *directly* to nest. Keep it a short leash. Somebody copy."

We arrive back at the lodge from a different direction than the one we'd left, which takes us through the makeshift kitchen. The kitchen staff is serving lunch and when they see us, I hear my new nickname "Bama."

"Yeah, yeah, it's all fun and games until somebody loses a trekker. Well not today y'all, so back to work!" Everybody laughs and pat our backs as we pass. In fact, I think they're enjoying this moment.

I love the Sherpa, and the porters, and the kitchen staff. They're all God's Guardian Angels for trekkers in their homeland. They see and embrace their roles fully; they are competent and focused while doing a seemingly impossible job. They're all somehow always at the right place at the right time.

I see Tenzing at dinner and ask if he heard about me getting lost. He cracks up and I assume that's a yes.

"Laugh it up Tenzing. Y'all are gonna miss me when I'm gone. I hope you do feel guilty."

He laughs but his reply is serious, "No, Suzanne, no. We won't lose you. Don't worry."

That's great news for me because, there ain't no mountain high enough, I can't get lost twice, on the way down.

Climb of Nangkar Tshang

180 degree views

Top of Nangkar Tshang; L-R Deming, Bikal, Teresa

Someone kissed your freakin face

At the top

L-R Mary, Teresa, and John

Lost and Found, Lost and Found; I'm far left

# 20

## Dr. Boo, the Walmart Greeter of the High Himalaya

*(Trek to Chukhung–15,518 ft. and Climb of Chukhung Ri–18,209 ft.)*

When we leave Dingboche, we hang a right and exit the Everest trail. The trek starts with a steep descent to the Imja Khola River. The tight trail winds through a rhododendron forest and after crossing the river, it directs us upward again.

We stop in the small village of Pangboche for lunch and Ruth buys a camelbak. A camelbak is a plastic bag held in the backpack that holds water and extends a drinking straw to the hiker. She hasn't been hydrating enough because she had to get her water bottle out of her backpack one-handed. She doesn't need help with anything, and even on these steep trails, she's asked for nothing. I hadn't noticed before, I'm gonna have to keep a closer eye on her.

I can't use my own camelbak because it's missing the piece that seals the bag. I know hydration is key so I'm trying, but to get to my water means getting someone to finagle the bottle out of my backpack, wait with me while I drink it, and then strap it up again. I'm not gonna do that. I'm not asking for help for things I consider baby shit.

John is walking with me and insists on carrying my water bottle. He doesn't trust my self-report of hydration, but he doesn't bust me out loud. The last time I try to assure him, he just looked at me and said, "I know." Then he smiled and kept my water. This guy misses nothing. I'm so grateful for John.

At dinner I laud John and swear, I'll do better on my own tomorrow. I point to a few engineer types in the group and ask for help to fix my camelbak. A kitchen porter overhears the conversation and asks to see the water bag. Soon he returns it fixed and ready to go. He carved a stick to slide over the bag and create a perfect seal. He saved me from some level of dehydration.

I thank him profusely and as he walks away I notice he isn't wearing socks beneath his sandals. Lhakpa is nearby and I ask him if the porter is sockless by choice. When he tells me it's probably not by choice, I go to my room and get two pair of my thickest and warmest. I take them to Lhakpa because I don't want to make the guy uncomfortable but Lhakpa suggests I give them personally.

I find the porter outside and hold the socks out, "*My* feet are cold, *because you're* not wearing socks. I promise they're clean."

His smile is wide but he's hesitant. I extend the socks further, "Please, they're not even mine. I took them from my best friend's kid and *he would totally want you to have them.*" He doesn't want to take possession of stolen goods, but when I extend them as if to drop them, his instincts take over and he holds them. Accepting the socks he bows his head and thanks me, "Dhanyabad, *Bama*."

I laugh out loud and he's confused. Yet I can't explain why "Dhanyabad, Bama" struck me so funny, other than it really surprised my mind. Hearing a new nickname that spread so quickly and thoroughly, and across language barriers. I assure him, "You're most welcome; it's my pleasure."

We head out early in the morning for our next stop in Chukhung, at over 15,500 ft. It's a shorter trekking day but it's strenuous. We arrive in the village early afternoon where we're greeted by the innkeeper's sons, three and four year-old, Paljor and Wangchu. It seems odd to see children here and they come across as wonderful novelty items. This harsh environment seems impractical and even dangerous to me. I flash to my childhood and hand me down motorcycles without helmets, swimming in Lake Tuscaloosa unsupervised, and driving various motorized vehicles without the governors my Dad always promised my Mom.

Again, shame on me. These children are *womb-safe* in comparison.

While we wait for room assignments, the children's soccer ball becomes a hit. Several from Asian Trekking, and a few from A+BC, showcase impressive skills. Julie, Andy, and Michael produce skills. I'm beginning to expect super-human endurance from the natives, but where is this reserve coming from with our people? Don't they know how hard this is?

We head to the tearoom for lunch and Justin breaks out his guitar. I'm sitting in his line of vision so he calls out, "Hey, Suzanne, I got one for you." I know after the first few chords we're about to sing, "Sweet Home Alabama." I see a map on the wall depicting our current location in Nepal, and I'm reminded of how far away I am from home. The song crescendos, "Sweet home Alabama. Lord I'm coming home to you."

I hear the small boys shriek with laughter as Dr. Deming turns one of them upside down.

Even though I'm drop dead tired, I'm trying to soak in every nuance. Some of the tearoom walls are glass, so I get unobstructed views. I'm hyper-aware of these majestic mountains, amazed at their beauty, and humbled in their presence.

After lunch, the younger boy greets me in the entryway, snorts, and spits a wad of blood toward my feet. He doesn't spit *at* me, but he clearly wants my attention.

I respond factually, "Yeah, that can't be good. But I know who can help you." I hold out my hand, "We're going to find Dr. Deming, O.K.? I think he's right outside." He takes my hand and we walk into the stone courtyard where indeed the doctor is enjoying the sunshine. As soon as I tell him about the bloody nose he gently scoops the boy up in his arms and while holding his head lower than his body, applies pressure to the bridge of his nose. The boy's calm, almost limp, in his sense of safety and comfort.

Dr. Deming responds to my nonverbal reaction, "He needed help, and he knew he could trust us."

Helping someone in need seems as natural and instinctive to him as breathing. He's got something very special in his DNA. Kind of like he's the cousin of a cousin of, I don't know, maybe, *Jesus*?

I wonder what it would have been like to have a loving, caring, and attentive father. I was unimportant to the point of invisibility to mine. He proved it more than once, but the first time I remember was when I was five.

Don usually picked me up from kindergarten on his way home from work every day around 3:30. On this particular day, he chose instead to go to his favorite bar, Jackie's Lounge, and drink.

I couldn't tell time yet, but it was getting dark and I was the last one left. When my mother arrived, she apologized profusely to the teacher. On the ride home, she fumed and used words she saves for when she's *super* mad. She could give a landlocked sailor a run for his money when she was *super* mad.

When we got home, Don was leaning against the kitchen counter eating a fried bologna sandwich.

She let him have it and he tried to stop swaying enough to focus on the tiny figure in the doorway. His eyes were bloodshot and watery and he slurred, "Well, whatever, or *everwhat*, she's fine. Aren't you Sister?" (Sister is the only name he ever called me.)

I wanted to scream at the top of my lungs, "No! No, I'm NOT alright! You left me and didn't even call Mama! I hate you! I HATE YOU SO MUCH!"

That's what I *wanted* to say, but I didn't. Instead, and with all the five-year-old gusto I had in me – I burst into tears.

I ran outside to find my dog, the one person I was positive would never leave me at kindergarten.

When I look back at Dr. Deming and the little boy, they're lying in the courtyard side by side, asleep. This little boy has grown up so loved and protected *he can fall asleep next to a stranger.*

I sit nearby and lean against the stone wall. Everything and everyone are safe and happy. I take tomorrow's itinerary out of my backpack and read,

"During our rest day at Chukung, our team will have an opportunity to climb Chukung Ri. The climb is not technical and should be challenging, but attainable, for anyone who's interested in making an attempt. From the summit of the peak, *you'll have extraordinary views of many of the tallest mountains in the world including Everest, Ama Dablam, and Lotsi.* The summit climb will take no more than a few hours."

Give me a break. I've done enough of these itineraries to know better. *"A few hours,"* it says. *"Should be challenging but attainable"* it says. That means it'll take most of the day and be the hardest thing I've ever done to this point in my life. Thank you, but I'll **pass.**

I rest my head against the wall and close my eyes. I take slow deep breaths inhaling crisp air and feeling the warm sun on my face. I'm reminding myself to be in the precious present and shortly, I'm able to forget about the pain and fatigue. I don't *feel anything,* but I *sense everything.* This time and this place are absolutely perfect in every way. I'll probably attempt to summit Chukung Ri tomorrow.

At dinner, we're told anyone that doesn't make it to the top of Chukung Ri tomorrow shouldn't attempt Imja Tse three days from now. He informs us that Imja Tse's base camp has been moved to a lower elevation, so the trek to summit will start from much further away. The addition of those extra trekking hours puts summiting *way* out of my league, so I let myself off the hook guilt-free.

But I'm committed to making great use of the day described as "optional." I'm thrilled at the prospect of sleeping in. I specifically remember, "Those not wishing to do the additional summits can lounge around sipping tea and playing cards." Me!!! I'm a tea-sipping, card-playing *fanatic*!

Before going to sleep, I happily make a request of Ruth. "Please wish everyone traveler's mercy from me, and no, I won't need a thing until everyone's back and lunch is cold."

The next morning, I wonder why someone's sitting on the edge of my bed, *talking*. I speculate Ruth forgot to deliver my message so I take the rolled up t-shirt off my eyes, and adjust to daylight. I remove one earplug, then the other, and the image begins to speak. I hold up a finger and eject my mouth guard.

We both laugh, but I'm just being polite, I'm not really happy to see him. This "optional day" is my *spa day,* and at 7:40 a.m., he's cutting into my "**me time**."

"Hey, what's up Doc?"

"Ruth said you weren't coming today. Do you feel alright?"

I sit up to assure him, "Yes, I do, thanks. It's just there's no way I can summit Imja Tse, so I won't worry about this one either. But, I'm gonna do all kinds of stuff from the 'optional day' itinerary!"

I've sprung to life quickly, but perhaps too quickly. He seems confused, "Don't you *want* to climb this mountain?"

Is this a trick question? No. No I do not want to. Don't get me wrong. I'm 100% blown away and appreciative of the view from *below*. But I don't want to climb anything. I don't want to have to step over my jacket to get to the bathroom.

But his manner is one of incredulity so I croak, "Of course I would. But unfortunately, the change in base camp takes me out of the game. *I've done the math, so I know,* I can't summit Imja Tse."

He doesn't waver, "Wait. How do you *know* you can't do it?"

I try to explain the *math,* "The change in base camp means adding another four to five hours past the longest and hardest day of trekking yet, and *that* day almost killed me."

"What do you mean? I don't understand your *math.*"

I try harder. "If you add up all the different hours from the last four days, then factor in altitude changes, plus the three to four hours added because base camp is now moved, it's …"

I've confused myself.

He gently encourages me, "*Take all the time you need* to get the math straight…but you may as well do it while you climb the mountain, right?"

I don't seem to have a leg to stand on so I suppose to myself, "Surely he's good at math, and I've come this far, I may as well keep drinking the Kool-Aid."

In short order I'm in the courtyard, suited up and ready to go. I've missed exercise and meditation so I retreat into earbuds as the last group departs. Hello Kitty plays songs I've never heard before and I just want comfort music; music I know by heart. What I hear is a sultry voice that just won a couple of Grammys. Adele's soulful when she asks, "Should I give up, or should I just keep chasing pavement, even if it leads nowhere?"

I ponder the question in a literal sense and conclude two choices; Up or down. Dr. Deming is behind me and I don't want to have to explain the *math*. I'm going higher.

Dr. Deming catches up and asks how I'm doing. Honestly, overall I'm great, but at the moment, I'm challenged for oxygen.

We walk for a while and the conversation, unlike the terrain, flows easily. I'm higher than birds fly so the air is rebellious in my lungs. I try to pant quietly and discreetly, as he politely asks thoughtful questions. I want to engage, I try to engage, but I can't. I can't freakin' breathe, and I'm not sure what comes after panting. I go blunt to the point, "Look Boo, the only interesting thing about me right now, I can't breathe. So I can't chit chat, sorry."

Damn, I just called him Boo. Need to edit better. He's chuckling as I apologize, "That's O.K., you can call me Boo."

I Shrug. "There's already too many Boos in this world. How about, *Dr.* Boo?"

"Yeah O.K., *Susannah Bama*, that works." He picks up his pace, leaving me content to walk alone.

I'm almost to the top and pause to catch my breath. I'm trying to take it all in, and this is *a lot* for all at once. I almost didn't climb this mountain. The mountain that lets me see every other badass mountain in the world from one spot. On the top of Tennessee's Lookout Mountain, you can see four states at once. I remember when that was a big deal.

I'm not to the top yet, but I'm already higher than surrounding peaks, and in a few yards or so, this mountain will end.

But there's no template in my own world to grasp, much less describe, this *now*.

When I reach the summit, *Dr. Boo* is there waiting with outstretched arms. I go to hug him, trip, and knock off his new cowboy hat. This man is constantly welcoming people to new and spectacular experiences, but this is what he gets for his efforts for me. It's windy and the right gust could put an end to his cool cowboy hat. I wonder if he'll accept a brightly colored woolen cap in the shape of a frog as a replacement.

He's not bothered in the least and I imagine him saying, "Welcome to Paradise. Come browse one of the highest mountains in the world. Soak up the views. Today the blue light special is 'Blessings from God, *no limits.*'"

I feel tons of gratitude for Dr. Richard Deming – *the Walmart Greeter of the High Himalaya.*

Trek to Chukhung

Soccer with the inkeeper's sons

Justin

In the Tea Room with Dr. Deming

$3 and worth so much more.

I don't complain about bad parking spaces anymore.

With Kathy, getting close to the ridge

Mary and John

There goes Dr. Boo's hat!

# 21

## The Yak Fest

*(Compassion is a Verb)*

The top of Chukhung Ri defies ocular confines. The weather is perfect and I can see multiple peaks from here. They confidently chat up familiar white clouds. The sun's light, the sky's color, and the air's crispness, they all align into perfection.

At 18,000 ft. we dance to Michael McDonald's version of *Ain't No Mountain High Enough*. In the spirit of transparency I'll clarify; by "we dance" I mean, we head-bob and disco-finger-point" for about thirty-six seconds. At this altitude, unnecessary exertion is masochistic, and that's not us.

As more of the group arrives I move to the side of the top and sit on a large rock. I'm absorbing this moment and when I see Kristin, I think about Emma. I feel overwhelming love for my daughter and a river of tears emerge. I didn't bring enough Kleenex for my constant dripping faucet of a nose, so I go for the cleanest shirtsleeve.

Something on the ground sparkles in the sunlight and I pick it up a small triangular rock. I'm still thinking of Emma and holding the small rock between my palms I pray, "Dear God, please bless Emma Claire with an abundance of love, and keep her always safe in Your Angel's wings."

After jotting my prayer on a scrap of paper, I roll the stone into it and zip them both away in my backpack.

After a glorious day full of natural highs, the balance of life creates an evening of ugly lows. The stars light the stage for what I call *"the yak fest."* On this evening our group single handedly wipes out the lodge with bodily fluids spewing from multiple orifices, and at this point, I may need to be medicated for an acute attack of ILS.

The sun is getting low as I sit outside the lodge with an ailing Leah, whom I've grown fond of in a short time. She's hunkered over a small pail trying not to throw up, and I ask her whether or not touch would be helpful. When I'm in pain, I don't want to be touched, or even looked at, so I'm cautious. I'm not sure if it's a learned reaction, but I do know we weren't coddled as kids. Unless an accident resulted in blood or bone, nobody made a big fuss. That went for emotional pain too.

My Mom had to go back to school and get her graduate degree to keep her job. Don's drinking was increasing, and he was unreliable at best. With two kids, she didn't have copious amounts of free time, so when she showed up at my kindergarten's Easter egg hunt, I was surprised and *elated*. Always beautiful and stylish, she walked into the classroom dressed to the nines, a perfumed goddess. Every child converged on her, but none dared approach.

Every child with a lick of sense kept a respectable distance, except the bane of my existence, *snot face Mary Alice*. She plowed her way to the front and looked my Mom up and down. Without hesitation, she climbed into Mom's lap and jabbed her stubby arms around her waist.

Because Mary Alice washed her face in her own mucous, and never washed her hands unless a teacher made her, I started the rescue. I started peeling her off, but my Mom stopped me, "No, Suzanne, it's O.K." She looked at Mary Alice, "She's adorable." Then she hugged that booger-eating, roly-poly back!

I lunged at Pig Pen and demanded, "Get off my Mama!"

Right after the word, "off" I knew rules had been broken, and I was gonna pay. Mom grabbed my arm and brought her face rudely close to mine. She whispered, (if whispering sounds like the low growl of a pissed bear) *"Leslie Suzanne, what's the matter with you?"*

I understood the concept of *rhetorical*, and kept quiet. She leaned a little closer, "You better *never* let me catch you acting like that again. *Do you understand me?"*

I nodded, but she tightened her claw around my arm, ever so slightly and deliberately, *"Do I make myself clear?"* That was the second phrase of ultimate intimidation. I prayed she wouldn't go to the third. *"We'll talk about this later."* Ouch, *there it was*! The single most intimidating thing a parent can say to a child. I lived in the moment and begged, "Oh please god *no*, not *later*. Kill me now cause later is too scary."

As kids, we were given instructions, then corrections, but if a third time was needed, we were given consequences. Learning curves were short and sweet because adults were clear and consistent. Now Mama was making herself very clear, but I'd known right from wrong all along. I attempted to mitigate the damage.

Sure, Mary Alice was annoying, but she was nice enough. She usually shared her contraband candy. She just did what came natural, climbed up in a lap and got embraced. It's not her fault I hadn't catalogued that as an option. I wanted to exercise that option now, but she wouldn't budge.

My insincere apology was delivered while she remained on the lap throne. With a poorly faked smile through a clenched jaw, I lied through a toothless gap, "I'm thorry, Mary Alith." Mary Alice shot me a look that screamed, "Ha ha loser, suck it!"

I didn't really care because Mary Alice had given me the gift of knowledge. Not once, but twice, she'd climbed into my Momma's lap and been well received. I now had reason to believe that I could just crawl up and sit *willy nilly* in her lap, and she'd think I'm adorable too. While this news was great, my Mama didn't raise an idiot, and my fear of rejection prevented me from ever attempting to sit uninvited in her lap.

I certainly don't mind coddling others and Leah tells me that touch is good so I pat her back, stroke her hair, and rearrange her coat, over and over. I hope it brings a small measure of comfort because I can tell, she's really hurting.

When someone mentions the adjacent lodge has toilets with actual seats, we go to find one for Leah. Much to our dismay, we realize that while there are in fact, seats on the toilets, the toilets have no plumbing. A toilet seat without plumbing is like winning the lottery in a bankrupt state—there are *no winners*.

I escort Leah back to the main lodge, to her room, and after tucking her in, I promise to check on her later. Her room is located right beside the bathroom and I think how smart Ruth and I were to choose rooms as far away from the bathroom as possible.

I make my way to the tearoom for dinner and can hear Carly as I approach. She's a 66-year-old cancer survivor with a horrible cough that's getting worse. My guess is pneumonia, but it's probably worse. Carly's roommate Julie isn't at dinner, so I go to check on her.

Their room is outside and the door is old, huge, and ill fitting. As I apply a gradual increase in pressure, the door scrapes, grinds, and squeaks until it opens. I don't want to scare her, so I yell loud enough to be heard over the protests of the door, "Hey Julie, it's just Suzanne. OMG, that was loud, I'm so sorry."

She makes a chuckle-snort noise and says, "That's fine, Bama, it happens every time the door opens. But I can't sleep with Carly's coughing anyway."

"No, I was talking about me. My ears are stopped up, so I may be yelling! Can I get anything for you?"

Her response is *immediate*, "Yes please, Dr. Deming."

Julie doesn't sound good, "Get Dr. Boo. O.K. I'm on it!"

The door reproduces the same god awful sounds and now it's fighting me back. We're jockeying for position and I'm painfully aware that every second I lose this battle, the temperature of the room drops by three degrees. I curse the door, "Damn you damn door," then remind myself to **quit yelling**.

I find the doctor on call and surprise, surprise, it's *Deming*. She becomes the next one on his list, so I relax, and let Julie go for tonight.

While I'm sorry people are sick, I'm happy to be in a position to help. Ready to call it a night, I take a step down the hall to my room. The smell of diarrhea and some combination of *death meets hell,* hits me in the face. The stench causes my eyes to burn.

I back pedal into the kitchen and when I find the innkeeper and his wife, I exhale, "Wow, I hate to bother you, but I think the waste paper baskets in the bathroom need to be emptied, maybe burned."

He doesn't speak much English but he's *mastered* sign language. He communicates emphatically by shaking his head back and forth and holding his nose. He uses his other hand and points at me.

"No, **not** *me*! NOT ME!"

His wife laughs, "Noooo, your friend."

"What friend? Oh my god, did they *die*? Who *died*?!"

His fingers spray outward to indicate vomiting. Then he turns his butt towards me and makes the same gesture. What the hell is he trying to say? His wife starts waving both her hands furiously in front of her crinkled nose.

Now, I understand and start to *howl!* I'm not laughing at the event, I'm cracking up over how they went about describing it. Language wasn't a barrier. But I need to know if someone *literally exploded,* so I head back to find several people in front of my room.

The attention is on Kim and Marilyn's room. They've both been sick and I hear Dr. Deming from inside the room, "We're gonna need new bed linens, and a new mattress. Actually, is there any way we can just get another room?"

Aww, hell no. Maybe this is payback for scouting the best rooms. I barrel out the front door waving my arms like windmills. John Richard is perched with his camera on the stone wall and asks, "Hey Bama, what's wrong?"

Ruth bursts through the door behind me and I point, "Ask her."

In stark contrast to the scene inside, the one outside is magnificent. John's Canon 7D is on a tripod focused on Lotsi. The camera is timed to take a picture every 15 seconds and the result is an incredible time lapse video. The clouds move in, out, and around the mountain top, while the stars dance and wait for the moon to show up and send them off to bed. The stars are mesmerizing.

Living in the country allows stars to shine unabated, and as a child, I spent a lot of time looking up and making wishes on them. These are the same exact stars decades later, only now I'm watching them from the other side of the world, and through the eyes of an adult. It feels greedy to make a wish on them tonight because I'm so abundantly blessed. Tonight as I gaze upward, I simply say, "Thank you."

Ruth and I take our last bathroom break outside in the fresh air. We're both wearing our headlamps although we don't need them. The moon is casting shadows as we walk. The bright orb looks so close I could probably touch it with a good running start. We walk far enough behind the lodge and out of sight to spots along a stone wall.

I notice a house at the base of the mountain. The windows glow with lamplight and it occurs to me, people really live here beneath this dancing sky. I wonder if they're immune to the surrounding beauty. There'd be no way to take Mother Nature for granted *here*, would there? The people that live here have to be hard workers. Do their hardships make them more present and grateful?

I'm aware I just made a judgmental assumption. I assumed people that live here consider themselves laden with hardships. What I consider difficult may be run of the mill to them. It's clearly a matter of perspective, and clearly, *my perspective is undergoing radical changes.*

Ruth's shadow moves and I hurry to catch up with it. Even though the night air is chilly, it's without odor. We hang out in the courtyard chatting with others watching Justin's nightly sing-along inside the tearoom. It appears the only people healthy enough to participate are from Nepal.

A sudden movement under the windows gets my attention. Andy's Dad has been sick and coughing, so Andy's brought his sleeping bag outside to sleep. But now he's shot upright and begun to projectile vomit. I'm less than a dozen feet away and start running when all of a sudden—*shwoop*—a Sherpa drops out of thin air, sans red cape. He grabs the back of Andy's coat and pulls him upward to make sure he doesn't choke. I grab Andy's collar and hold his forehead with my other hand.

He's hurling big time and I need to distract myself. I ask the Sherpa, "Seriously, where did you come from?" He shrugs and grins and I bet he knows we revere every single one of them. In similar superhero fashion Dr. Deming arrives taking Andy's head from me.

The dancing in the tearoom catches my attention again and I stand transfixed watching God's Guardian Angels of the high Himalaya. They're having a blast although they worked their butts off today getting us up and down the mountain safely.

The porters and kitchen staff always travel ahead of us and find enough flat ground on which to lay a tarp for a tablecloth. The center of each tarp is always lined with the same condiments of honey, sugar, peanut butter, salt, pepper, and powdered cocoa. All meals include a hot juice, soup, bread, vegetable, and protein. Afterwards, they clear and clean the dishes and eventually pass us on the trail heading to our evening lodge. They're usually well into dinner prep by the time we arrive at our destination.

Their responsibilities seem impossible to me so *I'm beyond impressed by them.*

The next morning I can't find my prosthetic breast. While the term sounds high-tech medical, it's simply a silicone gel form that goes inside the bra. I haven't had reconstructive surgery yet, and the right breast is half the size of the left one. Without the prosthesis, I have an uneven appearance. The inconvenience of having a free floating breast increases every time I lose it.

I find it under my bed and notice it's full of bubbles. Holy cow, the altitude is creating bubbles in the gel. The observation strikes me as particularly funny and I immediately think of a fellow patient I met during radiation. The one with the same name as my best friend, Martha.

Radiation Martha was a large, friendly woman in her late sixties who had lost her sizeable left breast in a mastectomy. She often made me laugh so I looked forward to seeing her every day. One day she pointed at the left side of her chest and complained, "I can't find a good enough boob filler for this side of my bra."

I must have looked confused because she opened her gown to reveal the big and the little of it. The left side of her chest was flattened with only scars to protrude. The right side was still sporting an enormous breast that childbearing, age, and gravity had *substantially* altered.

She hadn't found a good source to fill the left cup and her latest stab at symmetry was a tube sock filled with BBs from Walmart. She was at her wit's end when she said, "It ain't nowhere near big enough but I can't fill it no bigger 'cause it'll snap my strap. BBs would fly everywhere. Probably kill a few."

Her hands gestured the explosion of her left breast.

I cracked up, "Ahahaha Martha! I can see the headlines, "BB shrapnel kills and maims at local Radiology Clinic. Number of casualties unknown as efforts shift from search to recovery. Let's go to Ned, now on the scene ..."

Martha was laughing and getting worked up and egged me on,

"Yes, thank you, Bob. The Medical Director of the cancer treatment center gave us this statement, and I'm *almost* quoting, 'Radiation treatments will continue as soon as we can clear all the BBs out of the bleeping machinery.' As of yet, there's been no claim from any organization, so motive for the attack remains unclear. Back to you, Bob."

Doubled over in laughter Martha allowed her gown to separate again. I held up my hand to block the visual and suggested, "Dang girl, why don't you get a prosthesis?"

She'd never heard of such so I filled her in before my turn under the Lightsaber.

A few days later, Martha emerged from behind a dressing curtain with one hand behind her back and grinning from ear to ear. "Hey, Suzanne, close your eyes and hold out your hands!"

I extended a hand, palm up.

"No, *both* of them."

Something warm and heavy landed in my hands. I hadn't anticipated the weight and when I opened my eyes, I realized I'd almost dropped her brand new breast prosthetic.

She was animated, "Whoa, don't drop my *tiddy*!"

She retrieved her prize and lifted it into the air with both hands like a trophy. The gesture unfortunately allowed her robe to free-style open. Sometimes a moment unfolds into something more than interesting or amusing, more than surprising, and beyond downright funny. Sometimes a moment combines just the right amount of absurdity and spontaneity to surprise the mind to the point of hysteria. I live for such moments, and this was one of them.

I fell to the floor and grabbed my sides as the tech came in calling Martha's name. Martha addressed the tech as she stepped over me, "Ignore Suzanne, she's fine. *Now*, close your eyes and hold out your hands."

I laugh again recalling the event but I need to focus because I'm painfully slow in the mornings and I'm late for breakfast *again*. When I enter the tearoom Dr. Deming is standing in the middle, addressing the group. I pray he doesn't see me, but he looks right at me. I pray he doesn't stop talking, but he stops talking. I pray he doesn't address me, so of course, he addresses me, "Bama you missed what I just said, so I'll fill you in quickly. Some of us are leaving this morning for base camp; others are staying here another night."

Oh thank you Jesus; I needed this break SOOOOO much! He continues, "Some people need just a little longer at this altitude to acclimate." This man is a psychic god! He's so…he continues speaking and I die a little.

"Bama, you're going to base camp today." Using a thick Russian accent for emphasis he adds, "You're strong like bull."

No, wait! What? No, I'm not strong like bull. I'm weak like moth. This is *terrible* news and it's all my own fault. I've gone out of my way to convince him he's underestimated me. Is it wrong to fall on my knees and beg his forgiveness now? If I could, I'd beseech him, "I'm sorry I thought you were being an asshole back in Khumjung. You were just trying to offer me an easier journey. You were right, and as is often enough the case, I'm the queen of the wrong people. *Please, **please**, let me stay here.*"

But I can't ask that. Correction; I *won't* ask that. I'm fully aware, "Pride goeth before destruction, and a haughty spirit before a fall." I'll take pride and haughty spirit if I have to, but I'll NEVER be confused with ungrateful or self-entitled, so I acknowledge the decision. I try to infuse humor into my response and in my own best Russian accent I declare, "I may be strong like bull, but *I* give…"

***NOOOO****,* don't say it Suzanne! Don't say **MILK**; it'll come across as dirty!

I've already begun enunciating the "m," so I'm committed. Skid marks are inevitable as my big save goes off the rails. I gurgle loudly, "but I give …*MmmaahhHAANK!*"

I sounded like an over-stimulated goose. I dive into the nearest seat while Dr. Deming does a slow head shake. He doesn't know what *mmmaahhhaank* means, so he continues, "Because of medical concerns, Kim and Marilyn are being airlifted to Kathmandu. Three others are returning to Lukla on horseback, and we'll reunite with them there."

After Qigong, meditation, and a group picture, the ones with *bull strength* head off to Imja Tse.

On top of Chukhung Ri

Dancing at 18,000 ft.

L-R Judith, Dr. Deming, Me, Dr. Charlie

Here come the clouds

They're here!

John Richard creating an amazing nighttime video using stop motion photography

The one picture with the whole gang

# 22

# Goodbye to Florence Nightingale

*(Down for the Count at Base Camp—16,305 ft.)*

The majestic mountains east of Everest include the 22,000 ft. high Imja Tse, which translates into Island Peak, because when viewed from above, it appears as an island in a sea of ice. The trek isn't particularly hard, but at times the width of the path allows for only one. A misstep could result in a massive recovery effort.

After several hours of trekking the terrain has changed, and apparently so have my lungs, because it's getting much harder to catch my breath. The earth must be rotating at a weird new angle because I'm also getting disoriented and dizzy. I'm grateful when a break is called and start rifling through my backpack for a snack. I'm not hungry but I know I need to eat something, so I look for something salty. All I have is a short stack of Pringles potato chips so I eat them slowly, one at a time, which seems to be helping.

Michael plops down beside me and wants to know what I'm crunching.

"Nuttin, chow hound." I palm another chip.

"O.K. Bama, let's see it. What'd you have?"

"Shush. Be quiet." I give him half of my precious stack with advice, "Make it last." He pile-drives the entire gift down his pie hole in one reckless motion.

Someone yells at him, "Hey, Michael, where'd you get the chips?"

He looks at me and my gaping jaw and laughs, "*Bama* gave 'em to me."

I hit him with the empty Pringles can, "*Why*?" I'm distracted from his beating when someone announces, "Look who's coming!" In the distance porters round the bend bringing trays of cookies, and kettles of hot juice.

We begin passing through different basecamps and soon we arrive at our own. Some of the Sherpa and porters went ahead of us and have already set up basecamp in a valley between two large ridges. Two person, yellow-domed tents are scattered throughout with a large blue tent for dining, and a smaller green one to serves as the kitchen.

I should feel like I'm entering the gates of Heaven, but instead my mind is racing in a different direction, "Where do I get an aspirin, or a dozen? Why am I so nauseous? Is that my stomach I just heard? Did I buy enough toilet paper? How much is enough? How many rolls does Ruth have? Thank God for Ruth."

We go directly to the big blue dining tent because lunch is being served. Unfortunately the kerosene fumes from the heater makes me gag. For the first time on this trip, eating is a *serious* struggle. I fear whatever I put in my mouth will revisit, uninvited and explosively.

Even though it's cold outside I can't eat in the tent, so I stay outside. A couple of other down and out trekkers dine with me, each for their own intestinal reasons. The *unZen* is one of them. She looks thin, pale, and unwell. She leans against a big rock and says, "I can't even pretend to eat anymore." I'm growing concerned for her.

Someone comes with hot naan and fresh cut cheese (*hee hee*) and while I don't want it, I know that food + water intake = survival. It's been drilled into all of us by now. I eat all my ginger soup and one small bite of everything else on my plate.

As my food digests, my stomach complains. I stay put a bit longer because I'm afraid moving will make it worse. I look to the top of the ridge and wonder what's on the other side. I'll find out after a short rest.

As I head to my tent Justin arrives in basecamp. He trips, and when his head bobbles, he looks like a cartoon character. Laughing hurts my head so I hold back, but before he can fully correct himself, he trips again and his head bobs bigger. I can't help it now and burst out laughing. A sharp jab crosses my skull and I damn the pain to hell.

I have to stop every couple of steps to catch my breath and I don't seem to be moving forward. The ground is shape shifting and my gauge of distance and elevation are constantly wrong.

When I bend forward to enter the tent, my brain slams against my skull and I yell, "Aww, son of a ..." and grab my head. Standing back up, I squeeze my scalp tighter. I feel like I'm being lobotomized. I have to lay down right now, but I'm sure, I'll be better soon.

Time passes and life goes on, and then it's time to hang the prayer flags. I can hear several people right outside my tent and I want to join them and hang prayer flags too. The flags are being strung and crisscrossed to all corners of base camp. An image of my tie-dyed underwear flashes across my mind, probably because I have to go number two, *immediately.*

Outside, only sheer willpower and mad respect for Andy allow me to pass the large rock anchoring his tent. The next bathroom sized rock is castle like, circled in fresh yak poop. The moat makes me gag so I keep moving. The next respite is in the middle of the valley. It provides shelter from the group to the south, but leaves me exposed on all other sides as a constant flow of fit, handsome trekkers pass through our basecamp, returning to their own.

Modesty is a luxury now and after rallying out of my tent to make it this far, I unabashedly drop trou. I have a choice to make – dignity or clean underwear. I *don't* go commando and besides, we're all in the same boat so no one's paying attention. I have to be especially careful right now because I'm dizzy and unsteady. Getting rescued from a sunny-side up position would be stupid embarrassing.

It seems to take forever but when I finally get back to my tent, I pause. I wonder whether I can help with the prayer flags, or at least, sit outside and watch. In a nanosecond the answer presents itself – lay down before you fall down. I resign myself to a horizontal position and pray what I just experienced behind a rock was a one hit wonder.

Ruth and I rearranged the layout in the tent twice to minimize the angle and unevenness of the ground. We layered the pads we were given and I've fashioned most of my clothes into a mattress. I try to imagine I'm the Princess and the Pea.

It seems like days have passed but apparently it's only been a few hours. The sun must be thinking about setting because it's getting darker in here. Ruth breezes in to tidy up and asks if I'd mind if she opens the flaps for better lighting. When my eyes acclimate to the outside light I laugh out loud. This view *can't* be real.

The sun is getting low and the clouds are grounding. They're big, beautiful, and on the move as they glide around the base of the mountains. This is truly a magnificent day to be in Imja Tse base camp, and I have to experience this moment. I'm going to the top of the ridge even if it kills me.

Unfortunately, the ridge is on the other side of camp, and that feels a mile away (it's probably closer to one football field minus an end zone). I can't hurry and it seems like I'm stopping more than I'm starting. At this level, the air is authentically rarified and it makes me chase it. It offers a false promise though, because it can never be caught.

After about fifteen minutes I reach the top, and the beauty is *absurd*. The only thing that can limit this experience is my ability to absorb it.

The view on this side of the ridge is insane. At the bottom, a gorgeous blue glacier lake joins the bellies of two mountains. I want to freeze this moment in my mind forever. I'm seeing views that no one has seen in this way before, or will again. The light, temperature, even the earth's rotation, they've all come together to create this moment; a sensory experience that's utterly and completely mine.

The clouds are closer and there are more of them. The sun projects farewell rays that combine with the wind, temperature, and time, creating this perfect now. The cloud-floor alternates in yellows, pinks, and oranges; it reminds me of a 70's disco floor and I want to dance on it.

I'm suspended between heaven and earth and I see Michael on top of the ridge, a little ways north of me. He sees what I see, and he sees me seeing it too. We are both truly

*Strangers in a Strange Land*, trying to "*grok*" the magnificence of this time and place.

The sun is setting quickly and makes descending more ambiguous and tricky. By the time I micromanage each step back to base camp, I'm sick to my stomach. Someone calls my name from the dining tent, "Hey Bama, dinner!" I actually flinch and I want nothing to do with food. I can't eat and I may throw up.

I'm finding more and more things I can't do, and the operative word here is *can't*. I don't understand can't. Can't leaves room for helpless, and helpless leads to failure. Back in my tent, I lay helpless and failing. The feeling is a constant drumming in my head and draining in my heart. I'm smack dab in the middle of failing and I can't stop it. *I can't stop failing.*

Almost every part of this trip has felt impossible, but I've done it. Now, in my protective yellow dome, I'm right back at impossible. Have I been kidding myself? I don't think so because I *have* gotten stronger. I've gone beyond conscious agony more than once, pulled myself up by my bootstrap, and dusted myself off.

Lying here helpless and in pain causes me to feel small, and small allows old messages to resurface:

Alice fears, "People in the group will think I'm not tough. They'll see me as weak."

Logic counters, "Anyone that thinks that doesn't know me and is obviously a lousy judge of character."

Alice persists, "Dr. Deming will think it was a mistake to have included me."

I'm reassuring, "Please, don't even go there. He's been nothing but understanding and compassionate."

Alice worries, "Charlie Wittmack will think…"

Now Janis interrupts, "He can kiss a Himalayan mile of my ass. He should be worried about what I think.

Alice won't let up. "People back home will think …."

Janis fields the fear, "Ha ha, whatever I tell them. It's not like there's a *'fact checker'* that can bust me. Maybe I saved a whole village; I'm a hero, if I wanna be."

Alice isn't consoled, "Emma will think …" Once again the thought of my daughter grounds me. I know Emma's proud of me, irritated by me, tolerant and intolerant of me, all for different and largely valid reasons, *none* of which are correlated with my ability to climb a Himalayan mountain.

Breathing deeply, I can remember what I already know, a little better. And I already know that other's opinions of me may or may not be related to the truth about me. I am who I am – the good, the bad, and the ugly – regardless of how favorable or unfavorable someone's opinion might be. And the more solid point is that not everybody is thinking about me, so I needn't be so egocentric. The look on someone's face isn't always about me.

I have to use the bathroom again and I've held it as long as possible. Each trip has the same to-do list: put on shoes, find toilet paper, get a garbage bag, put on a coat, unzip the flaps, crawl out the flaps, re-zip the flaps, untangle myself from the tent's rope anchors, stand up, walk, breathe, oh god, breathe harder.

I have to go further out of camp for a good rock, and I have to hurry before this turns into a wardrobe disaster. Diarrhea is what we call it back home, but that's not what *this* is. Bowel movements at this altitude are puréed intestinal remains that make the domestic runs look polite and tidy. I'm not sure I have enough toilet paper for this diarrhea. I'm not sure if there's enough toilet paper in base camp for *this* diarrhea.

The whole bathroom expedition is exhausting, and back in the tent I feel even worse. The ground is most certainly colder and harder, and drama aside, *I'm freezing*. I look at Ruth's Antarctic quality bedding and roll over. As poor planning would have it, the sleeping bag I borrowed via Charlie is too small, and not rated for these low temperatures.

I hear Teresa laughing from the dining tent and I smile inside. Her final howl makes me want to laugh but it would kill my head! When she starts a fresh round my hands cradle my skull, and I feel immense gratitude for Teresa.

Voices speaking Nepalese approach my tent and one veers off to leave a single set of footsteps approaching and call out my name. It's Tenzing with an offer of dinner. When I decline all offers of food or beverage he hesitates, but says O.K. and leaves.

My thoughts have a similar strand like, "ways Tenzing is an amazing Sherpa," and "what really is a Sherpa?" and "are they genetically different than the average Nepalese?" and "do…?" I hear him call my name again and I answer, "Yes Tenzing?"

"May I open?"

"Yes, of course." Oh god, help me, I'm gonna have to sit up.

When he hears me groan he protests, "No, I'll bring to you."

"O.K., thanks a lot. Bring what?"

He extends himself far enough into the tent to hand me a piping hot cup of garlic soup, crackers, a spoon, and napkin. I thank him and I'm able to drink almost half of it. The food is needed though unwanted. Worse still, I have to accept help from others. I'm much better at giving than receiving.

Exhaustion sidelined me for a second early in the trip, but *that* was baby shit. I'm head-butting a whole new level of suffering. I was so happy to have helped my fellow trekkers last night at the yak fest, but now it's crystal clear, I have to say goodbye to Florence Nightingale

Trekking to Imja Tse basecamp

Michael hoovering my Pringles; Tenzing far right

The last corner into basecamp

Pareshaya Gyab 16,305 Ft.

Imja Tse

Suzanne Link

The view of all views - on top of the ridge

The clouds rolling in

Suzanne Link

When the sun sets

# 23

# What Fresh Hell is This?
*(That moment you realize, "I could die here.")*

The next time I see Tenzing is in the morning during breakfast time. He comes to check on me and I assure him I'm fine. When he returns with a plate of breakfast, I'm more honest, "I can't eat food. I can't eat anything. But dhanyabad *a lot*."

He keeps the tray offered forward until I take it from him. I thank him again but as soon as he walks away, I ferry the food through the tent and out the other end. The odor lingers and I almost gag.

At lunchtime the entire scene repeats itself, although it's shortened when I accept the tray sooner. Again, I beeline it out the back flap, but my breakfast tray is in the way. Passage is held up by a large rock. I push everything as far away as I can and while I can't hide the trays, my intentions are obvious.

Chatter increases as the second group of A+BC folks arrive from Chukhung. Soon I hear the sound of rock crushing beneath boots. Coughing arrives before the boots and when they catch up, I hear "Suzanne?"

"Yes?"

"It's Carly. It looks like you're getting a new roommate."

I hear the sound a pressure cooker makes when it's too full of steam. I may literally explode. My butt already has. I can't sit up or even move without severe head pain, and most importantly, I'm in an active struggle to stay off an emotional ledge.

Carly's been sick for days. It sounds like double pneumonia, *squared*. Her coughs are loud, long, and constant. Yesterday, Dr. Deming told her to stay in Chukhung but she wouldn't hear of it. She wanted to come to base camp and so here she is, AMA, right outside my tent (AMA – Against Medical Advice).

Ruth moved her sleeping bag into Andy's tent a short time ago, concerned she'll disturb me when she gets up at 1:00 a.m. for the summit. I told her that was completely unnecessary, but she insisted. Andy's tent was for him and his Dad, but his Dad had the good sense to take a horse down to Lukla yesterday.

This tent isn't big enough for a second deathly sick person so I tell her, "There's a mistake because Ruth hasn't moved out forever. Who told you to come to this tent?"

"Ruth told me, at lunch. But I'll go ask Dr. Deming."

Ruth told her to come take her place in our tent? I don't believe it.

Soon Dr. Deming comes crawling in. He sees the look on my face and before he can close the flaps, I'm explaining why someone with pneumonia shouldn't be a roommate. He doesn't think she's contagious but I'm not buying it. "You can't *know* that. There's no *lab* for testing." I point toward where I imagine Carly's standing and start to shake my head an emphatic *no*.

BAD MOVE. The pain sears and makes my eyes water. I vice-grip the top of my head and cradle it hard. Dr. Deming shows compassion and keeps Ruth in our tent, and gets Carly one of her own.

Next is the Relay for Life followed by a blessing from a Buddhist monk. I want to do the Relay for Life. I want a monk's blessing. He's gonna finish the service with a shot of scotch, or whiskey, or something high proof. I want a shot of something, and I'd offend a few Commandments for a bottle of it. Obviously, I *need* a monk's blessing.

Even though I can't be a part of it physically, I can hear sounds from the Relay for Life — Justin's guitar, occasional laughter. Then suddenly several people gasp. The silence is broken by a woman's voice. I hear her say the words, "just fainted" and "I'm positive, I'm O.K." It occurs to me that this is definitely *not* a good place to get sick.

I want to be a part of the activities but I'm flat on my back. However, my thoughts are standing up and I think about Emma. I know it's twelve hours earlier in Charlotte, but I'm not sure what day of the week it is, here or there. If it's a weekday, she's in school, a high school senior who's going to graduate early, in January, in less than 90 days.

Oh no, absolutely not. I can't think about Emma. She's always been so strong and independent. If my breath hiccups, I'll cry. No, I can't cry! My head will explode and that'll be a sure sign of HACE.

I warn myself to keep it together, "You know how to do extreme, and this is extreme fringe. This is *Wittmack/Deming extreme fringe.*"

Now, everyone's right outside my tent learning to rappel. Ruth is first up and while rappelling with two hands is hard, one handed seems reckless.

I hear Lhakpa request a Sherpa harness Ruth to him and when the Sherpa turns out to be Tenzing, I'm completely relieved. I trust everyone with Tenzing. I may trust everyone named Tenzing.

I wanna learn to rappel but my hands are so swollen I couldn't hold the rope. I must be retaining a small water tower throughout my body because I feel bloated. It doesn't matter because there's not a snowball's chance in hell I can summit tomorrow. My headache is worsening, and a strange abdominal pressure is forming an angry vortex to my anus.

I try to distract myself by thinking and so I think about things going on back home. If I were there, I'd be knee-deep in Alabama football. We have a shot at the National Championship again, for the third time in four years – *unprecedented* success in the BCS era.

BFF Martha visited in October, during my third round of chemotherapy. I was bald, 206 pounds, and having a hard time reminding myself, *this isn't the woman I've become.*

Before the Alabama vs. Tennessee game we went to the grocery store for more of my grazing needs. On the way we saw people alone and in small groups walking on the sidewalk. They were mostly dressed in pink, and many wore bright costumes and decorations.

A health station was set up in the neighborhood elementary school's parking lot. It was the Avon 39 Mile Walk for Breast Cancer.

As we stood in the bright sunshine cheering them on, I had to remove my scarf because of the heat. I stood there, radiant in all the consequences of my cancer, feeling supported, loved, and so very blessed. Some walkers stopped and hugged me; some became too emotional to even look at me, but I felt connected to every one of them.

What would Martha say if she were here right now? Ha ha, that's funny because Martha would never be uninformed enough to be in *any* base camp. But, part of her believed this was something I needed to do, and could do, although I bet she's scared shitless for me. I'm O.K. with that because I haven't completely moved past the whole Lukla thing.

Repelling lessons over, a kitchen porter brings me with hot soup. I'm glad it isn't Tenzing because I don't want to feel guilty all over again. I'm glad he doesn't know what deceptive steps I've been forced to take.

I thank the Sherpa and ferry the bowl of soup out the other end of the tent. This time, it fits easily outside and I realize the other trays are gone. Aww, man, I sure hope Tenzing doesn't know.

Soon I hear someone approaching and I freeze. Please, *oh please*, don't let it be Tenzing. The footsteps stop and Tenzing calls, "*Bama.*"

He's always called me Suzanne, but now, he's almost singing Bama.

"Yes Tenzing?" He pops his head through the tent followed closely by a full tray of food. He really wants me to take it and he seems *assertively* friendly, downright happy in fact.

I don't want the food, but of course, I take the tray and make polite chit chat. I start to get uncomfortable when he doesn't engage in the small talk. I thank him again but he doesn't move or blink. I wait and wait, and I smile and smile, until I *can't* hold eye contact any longer. I look down at the mountain of food on the tray, and my mouth twists as my tongue threatens to swell up and choke me to death.

I look back at Tenzing and the look on his face is unnerving. He slowly leans forward *just a tad*, then he *almost* smiles. I know, **I'm so busted**. He knows I'm a lying sack of shit and I bow my head low, until I can't stand the silence any longer. Guilt propels the apology, "Look Tenzing, I'm so sorry. I'm an honest person and I feel so guilty. I just couldn't eat or smell anything. I *really* couldn't. Do you understand?" He nods that he does.

"Do you forgive me?" He nods that he does, but the windows to his soul still politely chide me. I test him by offering the tray back, but he doesn't move a muscle.

Maybe if I make him feel sorry enough for me, he'll move on. "It's just that it's been so hard, you have no idea. My head and my stomach..." He's perfected his poker face and he's not leaving until he *sees* me eat. I give a last try, "O.K., you're right. You're *absolutely* right. I have to eat and *I promise I will*. Namaste, O.K.?"

He semi smiles and changes positions to get more comfortable, "O.K. good *Bama*."

Damn it he's still calling me Bama. My look is one of genuine helplessness and despair and he pauses for a second, then pointing to the potatoes, he holds up three fingers. I've engaged in deceptive behavior including avoidance, evasion, and lying. I owe him this so I take a deep breath and admit defeat. "O.K., we'll do it your way, but it's gonna take a while."

His shrug indicates he accepts my terms, *and* he's got all day. I take a bite of potato and it hangs out in my mouth too long. When I get the gumption to swallow it, it goes down hard.

Tenzing talks to someone outside the tent so I take a smaller, quicker bite. He looks back into the tent and says, "Nice try."

Once he's satisfied I've eaten three of his normal size bites, he makes closure with the whole thing by taking the tray. When I get him the full bowl of soup recently transported out the back of the tent, he rolls his eyes.

"Hey, you said you forgive me. Don't make me cry dude."

He gives up his mock disappointment and I hope he's sincerely not upset. I get the all-clear signal when his smile works itself into the laugh his eyes initiated a long time ago. It's at this moment that I realize what it's like to have a *caring* brother.

As he leaves I admit, "I know I've blown all my credit points, but could you, would you, keep an eye out for Ruth tomorrow?"

"Yes Suzanne, you're not to worry. It's O.K."

Ruth gets back and wastes no time getting into her sleeping bag because they're heading out at 2 a.m. I lie here with no idea who will summit, or even make an attempt. I know I'm not, so I can't wait for Ruth to get the hell out of here, so I can get in her sleeping bag. I'm so thankful basecamp was set up at this lower elevation because this is as cold as I can go.

I wait impatiently for the 1:00 a.m. wake-up call when the chef will bang on a pan to call forth the explorers. Time seems to be at a standstill, and when he finally pot-clangs for breakfast, I jolt upright. My skull gets pierced by a thousand ice picks, my eyes fill with water, and nausea threatens to be the asshole cherry on top. This isn't a headache. This is whatever happens when the skull starts cracking.

As soon as I'm able to catch my breath, I get back on task and shake Ruth, "Ruth, it's time. The pot rang, so you need to wake up and get going." She barely moves so I raise my voice a little, "Did you hear me? Focus Ruth. You know how you hate to be late." She takes a long stretch and I try to extend my patience, "Look Ruth, don't think they won't leave somebody in basecamp. They're gonna leave *you* if you don't *hurry*!"

On her way out I wish her well, "Have fun, be safe, and 'Billy don't be a hero!'"

She kisses me on the cheek while folding her sleeping bag around me and promises, "I'll be careful. I love you too." I figure I have an hour or so before I need to start praying for them, so maybe I can help myself in the meantime.

The hurting in my chest climbs into my throat and I want to cry, but I don't know why. I don't want to meditate because I can't close my eyes; I get dizzy and more nauseous. I need to gain control.

My mind flashes on the plane crash and the 19 people that lost their lives. Sixteen were trekkers headed out to make a dream of a lifetime come true. They went from euphoria, to death, within a few terrifying minutes.

The cotton in my chest is getting thicker and I need more air. The sensation causes a sharp inhale, and forces a small groan. I want to *let it all out* right now. I wanna bawl like a baby, but at this point, I fear I lack the same level of coping skills as a baby.

My mind flashes on how difficult yet amazing this trip has been. I'm aware it's the disease of cancer that got me here.

My mind flashes on my cancer journey.

My mind flashes on the people I'm most grateful for as a slide-show plays across the dome of my tent.

My mind flashes on …too much at once. I need the head throbbing to stop. I need to chill out so after about an hour of internal warfare, I start meditating. I rest my headlamp on my stomach and focus on the yellow circle it casts on the ceiling.

Slowly profound understanding shifts my core and I come to know, or maybe just accept, what I've known all along.

My biggest fear isn't of flying. My biggest fear isn't of dying. My biggest fear in life, is of not being good enough. I need to be good enough, to live fully and authentically, *without fear or shame.*

My life has been about that which I've struggled most to overcome. Hands-down I've struggled most to overcome *me*! I've been determined not to let my fears and weaknesses define and control me.

My imaginary bumper sticker reads, "God grant me the serenity, the courage, and the wisdom, *to overcome ...* **ME.**"

I need to be done with so much feeling for a while, so I distract myself with a little smack talk. For the *winners* about to summit I'm like, "Hey, y'all. Just so you know, there ain't no prizes on top. No gifts to unwrap. There ain't no steak dinner up there; probably won't be no hot juice. Oh look, what's this? Hot juice? That's right, we got lots' a hot juice in base camp."

I feel a spasm deep in my intestines. I went from wiping to dabbing a long time ago, so with toilet paper in hand, I head out to moon unsuspecting trekkers.

*What fresh hell is this?*

Hanging the prayer flags

Learning to repel

Relay for life

Amazing photography Andy!

# 24

## My Most Successful Failure Yet

Ruth turned back for basecamp at crampon point. She's not reckless and made a difficult but wise call. I'm positive that if she'd had a designated Sherpa of her own, she could have summited.

Now that she's back I have to relinquish her sleeping bag. Those few hours of warmth were beyond my wildest dreams of comfort. Now it's back to teeth-chattering, body-jerking freezing. Screw this. Andy's tent is vacant so I go and crawl into his sleeping bag, a waiting cocoon of warmth.

Andy's Dad was one of the three that left Chukhung heading back to Lukla on horseback. I'm moved by the parent/child duos in our group, and while I'm positive my Mom would never try something like this, I wonder if my Dad would have.

It seems strange to me, but I really wish my Dad were here.

Don died of a massive heart attack—his first—when I was 19 and he was only 46. I was a sophomore in college.

Turtle, drove me to the hospital where we entered a private waiting room in the ER. I saw aunts and uncles, a couple of my Dad's friends from work, and my *paternal* Grandmother, Mama Hoggle.

The emergency room doctor appeared in the doorway and after scanning the room he fixed his gaze on Mama Hoggle and me, "I'm very sorry to tell you, but he's gone." I was too shocked to react. Sure there'd been times as a child I'd wished him dead, but not anymore.

The doctor said another sentence or two, then offered, "If anyone would like to see him, I can take you now."

I shot up, "I do. I'd like to see him."

The doctor knew I was Don's daughter and stalled while Mama Hoggle begged me, "No, Shoog, don't."

Turtle stepped in and checked with me, "Floss, are you sure?" I nodded yes so he looked at the doctor and said, "O.K., let's go." Three years later Turtle would walk me down the aisle at my first wedding, and say something very similar, "You know Floss that you don't have to do this. We can walk it down the aisle, or we can walk it out the door. You make the call."

Our entrance into the triage room caused an immediate cessation of activity. A nurse pulled back the curtain revealing my Dad, bloated and blue on a stainless steel slab. She guided me closer to the table, then stepped back.

Vomit in the corners of his mouth edged purple lips. I looked at his arm. This arm had been a strong boulder that had hurt my mother, and caused tremendous fear in me. But it had been strong in good ways, too.

This arm helped him design, build, and fix anything and everything. There was nothing he couldn't do. He could fabricate anything with master precision as a highly respected machinist.

He designed and built the system that supplied our house with natural spring water.

He built a patio with a brick barbecue pit and extended walls for planters. That was HGTV before its time.

He built a pea shelling machine and elevated himself to Wylie Coyote Genius to my brother and cousins and me. We didn't have to spend hours shelling purple-hull peas anymore.

He skinned, cut, and packaged deer meat.

He was athletic and had played multiple sports. He loved Alabama football, fishing, motorcycles, and of course and above all …drinking.

I touched his arm and it was hard and cold, and it was dead. I looked at his dead hands and wanted them to wake up so they could create more amazing things. I looked at his boots, completely still and knew they'd never walk again. His boots were dead too.

I'd often viewed this man as the devil, now I just saw my Dad, and I wanted him back.

We'd started to develop a relationship and I had real hope. I'd done everything possible to get us this far. I'd taken a ridiculous amount of responsibility for him. When I was 16 he had a drunk driving accident that landed him in the hospital for a week, and then one of many extended stays in rehab. I'd pick up and cash his paychecks, then I'd take the money to his various creditors with promises to return in two weeks with more.

In the better times I'd make dinner dates and though he was often a no-show, when he did make it, we always had a good time. I'd hoped that over time, I'd become visible to him.

Now I felt gutted and frozen and while I could have cried in an instant, I wouldn't dare let myself. No, this setting was far too dangerous for raw emotions.

From behind, Turtle checked on me, "Floss, you O.K.?"

I turned around, "Yes, sir." I looked back at the dead person on the table, at my *Daddy*, and said, "I'm ready to leave now, please."

He walked me out the closest exit even though a sign on the door read, "Employee Exit Only." As he opened the door, he mumbled, "My ass."

When we got in his truck, he asked, "Where do you want to go? It's your call."

"Home. I wanna go home." Leaving the parking lot, Turtle took a right onto Paul "Bear" Bryant Drive and I exhaled. When we got on 82 West, my eyes filled with tears. After turning onto Watermelon Road, I began to sob.

My father's passing left me with conflicting senses of peace and grief. All chances for an adult relationship were gone. Sigmund Freud said, "I cannot think of any need in childhood as strong as the need for a father's protection."

That failed relationship left a hole in me.

In base camp I'm loving the warmth of Andy's sleeping bag, but way too soon he calls me name, "Hey, Bama, how's it going?" Andy is one of the two cancer survivors able to summit Imja Tse and I imagine he's beyond exhausted.

I head back to my tent where Ruth, already rested, is gone. Bending over to enter sends shock waves throughout my head and I clearly hear Martha, "The other one is **HACE**. That's High Altitude Cerebral Edema; that's when there's *fluid on your brain*. It feels like a vice-grip on your skull. These are both very, *very* bad ..." Oh dear god my brain is swelling out of my head. *MAYDAY* ...somebody, anybody!

I'm too unsteady to leave the tent for help so I'll have to wait for the next passerby. Luckily for me it's soon, and it's Tenzing. I begin, "I'm not sure Tenzing, but I may have altitude sickness so would ..." He holds up a hand and darts out.

Almost immediately the doctor's tripping into the tent and falls over me onto Ruth's side. I warn him, "You better not get your yak poop boots on that sleeping bag; it's Ruth's."

He's still focused on why he fell into the tent and wants to know, "Why are you coming and going out of the *back* of your tent?"

It has been unusually hard to get in and out of the tent because the front opening is small and high, but the one at the back is obstructed by a big rock. That end is good for nothing. You can't even hide food trays there.

Once I understand his point I admit, "It's really only been a problem for me. It's nothing for Ruth. She Spider-Mans in and out of everywhere."

He laughs and sprays a little.

I beg him, "No, stop it, you don't understand! I *can't* laugh because I don't have any more clean underwear. I've had to make *hard choices* to keep clean underwear!"

He can't wait and launches into a story about the time he tried to get out of a tent to a bathroom. Long story short, he didn't make it so he ended up under a full moon, in a river, washing away the consequences. I hold my head and he knows how bad it hurts when I laugh, but his sense of humor is getting in the way of his compassion. He seems to fight his own battle with ILS.

I plead with a hint of authoritarianism, "Seriously though, *listen*. I'm pretty sure I have altitude sickness because of my head, but *I'm positive* I have a *chapped ass*. I went from wiping to dabbing a long time ago. Dude, I need help."

He cracks up and eagerly gives me a tiny white pill. I swallow it without question. He wants to know why I haven't said something before now, and I take 100% responsibility for not being proactive. I've always had a high tolerance for pain, and when paired with my oversensitivity about being a burden, *I was stupid*. I admit I waited too long to ask for help.

I redirect the subject when I ask him, "Where was this little pill yesterday? Is this payback for the Carly thing?"

He laughs but goes right back to the subject, "Are you trying to kick *yourself* off the island?"

"No, I'm not. I swear. But this one's definitely on me." I broke my promise to him after bragging about how proactive I am in self-care. What happened this time? My heart sinks a little: Because this time self-care included *asking for help*. I'm beyond ready to put that issue to bed. I let my struggle become dangerous before I could see it for what it was. Regardless of my intent, I was irresponsible.

But to give a little credit where is due. I kicked that whole 'opinion of others of me' thing to the curb. Soon I'm drowsy, and for the first time since arriving at base camp, I sleep. I sleep for hours.

By dinnertime my brain must be smaller. I have a new definition for *headache*, so I know, this isn't one. I'm so much better now, I'm practically brand new. Outside I can stand, stretch, and finally, take in base camp. The air is crisp and cold as the sun hugs the mountains.

On the way to the dining tent, I walk through a circle of Asian Trekking staff and I hear someone say, "Look, there's Bama! Welcome back!" I hear the sentiment repeated and then the question, "Where have you been?"

I see the Sherpa that lost and found me twice and point at him. "Ask Radar. I bet *he* knows where I've been the whole time!" Everyone erupts and Radar walks over extending a high-five.

When I enter the dining tent I'm hit with smell of kerosene, but this time I can take it. I still can't eat much, but getting to see my friends during dinner is great. Too soon, too tired, I head back to the tent. I carefully watch every step I take even though the ground is brilliantly lit. I stop to breathe in the moment, and any extra air I hope is hanging around, and I look to the sky. Laughing in the sky's face is becoming a thing for me. Once again, I laugh out loud at what I see.

These are the biggest stinkin' stars I have ever seen, and this is the most beautiful, magical, and wonderful place on earth. I feel small and enormous all at once. I'm grounded but I can fly. Wow, wow, wow.

Anne Lamott gives a perfect explanation for the word "wow" in her book *Help, Thanks, Wow: The Three Essential Prayers*.

"And then there are the uppercase "Wows" that occur by having one's mind blown by the mesmerizing or the miraculous. When we are stunned to the place beyond words, when an aspect of life takes us away from being able to chip away at something until it's down to a manageable size to file it nicely away, when all we can say in response is "*Wow*," that's a prayer. What can we say beyond Wow, in the presence of things so glorious or magnificent they can't have originated solely on this side of things?"

I marvel at the author's wisdom because she nailed this moment for me. I feel complete peace and now, the words come out loud, "*Wow, wow, wow.*"

When I return to the tent Ruth is busy packing and announces, "We have to repack our ice picks and crampons." Her energy is serious and focused, but mine is *super-happy-chill*. "No Ruth, not me, I'm leaving this shit here. I'm not schleppin' it another *inch*."

She doesn't know about my conversation with Dr. Deming, and she isn't sure how to react.

"No, as a matter of fact, maybe somebody should tell Deming how inconvenient it was to haul this shit around in the first place. Go tell him and wave Stumper in his face while you do it."

She's shocked and her eyes are wide. Dang, I hope I didn't go too far. "Hey Ruth, I'm just messing with you. Dr. Deming said for us to put the stuff outside **either** end of our tent, and they'll take it from there. Hahaha, I wish you could have seen your face!"

She doesn't exactly laugh, so I make a note to myself; stop winding Ruth up. *You're probably not as funny as you think you are.*

Summit of Imja Tse

Summit of Imja Tse

Summit of Imja Tse

# 25

## It's All Down-hill from Here

*(Descent to Dingboche—14,468 ft.)*

As the morning sun greets us I feel human again. I've delivered my duffle bag early, and for the first time since arriving at base camp, I'm able to sit in the dining tent and eat a full meal that includes a hard-boiled egg, oatmeal, and naan. I still don't like the gas smell, but I can easily tolerate it.

Immediately after breakfast Judith leads us in Qigong. I'm enjoying every word she utters and every move she makes, when all of a sudden, there's a commotion behind me. The *un*Zen is on the ground. She fainted and she looks terrible, ghostly pale and thin. She comes to and insists she's O.K. She admits she hasn't been able to eat or hydrate properly, and oh boy I relate! I feel complete empathy and sympathy, and I'm nervous for her. She proclaims she's O.K. but what if she's as bad as me in asking for help? I have to accept that she isn't the first to faint and rally, so if she isn't concerned... But as for me and my healthy intestines and my normal size brain, we're headed south!

The descent to Dingboche is relatively easy, and within a few hours I'm sitting on the lunch tarp, *hungry*. That baby breakfast is long gone and my body wants to make up for lost meals. I *need* food.

Several people haven't made it down yet and Teresa announces, "We're waiting on them for lunch."

No way. I need to eat *now*. "How much longer do you think they'll be?"

"I'm not sure, but probably within an hour."

"Whoa, as in *60* minutes?"

"They'll be here soon enough, Bama."

I look through my backpack but I don't have food. I can see the kitchen staff has a lot of food at the ready and I keep my eye on it. Five minutes later I ask Teresa, "Is it *absolutely* necessary to wait for *everyone* before we eat?"

"Lunch isn't ready."

There's no way I'm getting into a debate with her over what constitutes a *ready* lunch and *a lot* of minutes go by before I suggest, "Maybe we could all just get soup? There's *always* soup, and the soups always ready."

She looks at me and walks to the other end of the tarp to retrieve her backpack. She takes something out and on the return tosses it to me, "Here, try not to die."

It's the packet of crackers she got yesterday in a lunch kit on the top of Imja Tse. Yes, Teresa was one of the eleven, and one of only three females, to summit!

I protest that I don't want to take her special crackers, "They're just crackers. Eat 'em."

I whisper, "Yes, ma'am." O.K. I admit it. I love and fear her equally. I may be inclined to a sort of worship.

When others begin to groan about getting hungry, I get nervous and intervene, "They'll be here soon enough. Teresa gave me some Imja Tse crackers, delicious and filling." I make a quick hand-off and lay low.

While we wait Judith and I talk about avalanches. Seeing them in the daytime from afar has been thrilling, but hearing them at night at basecamp was unnerving. Avalanches rumble then roar, and their ripple effects are unpredictable and dangerous. We agree that basecamp was exceptional and exciting for many reasons, in many ways.

The rest of the day's trek is mostly downhill, which is aggravating my lower back. My left knee has periodically been a problem since its initial blowout in San Francisco's Chinatown at 23. Then there was the rollerblading fiasco on my 31st birthday. So I'm *always* careful with my back and left knee, but my *right* knee has never been a problem. Now every step creates the same unrelenting cycle of pain, and I have to go slower and slower.

By the time I arrive at the Lodge in Dingboche, *both* knees hurt like hell. We gather in the tearoom, of course, but this particular one is on the second floor up the steepest, most narrow set of stairs ever created. Every painful step screams, "Mayday!"

As we wait on room assignments, John Richard walks around and asks people to describe their favorite part of base camp while videotaping their responses. When he reaches me, I keep it short, "I don't know. I didn't see it." When I'm in physical pain, I don't like to be touched, looked at, or talked to. I'm in *a lot* of physical pain right now so it's good and right that John keeps moving.

My room is just outside the main lodge along the courtyard, but it takes me forever to get down the steps. By the time I get to the room, Ruth is already there. Tenzing enters with a duffle bag and automatically starts to place it at the end of my bed. He stops suddenly and moves it over, to the end of *Ruth's* bed. What the hell?

He sets about his routine, setting it facing outward, loosening the straps for easy opening, making life good and right for someone, who is *not* me! Ruth's bag now has a red bandana tied to it and she's thrilled, "Oh good that worked. I saw you had a red bandana on yours, so I put one on mine too."

Where the hell did she get a random red bandanna? Mine was a gift from Martha on my 24th birthday. I wore it around my wrist until excessive nose wiping retired it to my duffle bag for easy identification. Ruth tying a red bandana to her bag would be a wonderful idea if it weren't such a *horrible* one, so I jokingly poke at her, "Are you poaching *my* Sherpa?"

A porter enters the room and tosses a bag in my general direction. He adds a kick spin that causes the duffle to land *near* the end of my bed, *almost* facing forward. He tips his head and bolts and I look at Tenzing and Ruth. The expression on my face causes them to laugh and Tenzing heads towards my bag. I cut him off and point a warning finger, "I see how it is. Don't even think about it funny Sherpa man." I can hear him still laughing as he crosses the courtyard.

After finding clean-*ish* clothes and scraping together shower supplies, I go to find the lady to pay for a shower. *Mercifully* she's downstairs in the lodge's entrance. I pay her and get super-excited when she informs me the person in the shower is almost finished.

Hurrah, I'm next! I lean against the wall facing the bathroom and get excited about *hot water* and *cleanliness*. My hair's disgusting and I'll get to wash it. I don't care what it looks like, I just want it clean. My hair isn't a big deal anymore.

# A Random Buzzard In Kathmandu

I didn't want chemotherapy to take my hair but my oncologist said it would start to fall out two weeks after the first round. I couldn't control my hair's demise, but I could control the bon voyage party.

A friend wanted to take me to her stylist and get me "the most adorable super short haircut ever."

Why would I want to watch the most *adorable ever* fall off my head? No thank you.

But her offer gave me clarity; I had to self-inflict a haircut so horrible that I'd *want* it to fall out. Challenge accepted. Brad and Emma don't always share my *pioneer* spirit so several days before my first treatment, I snuck into the bathroom to put my hair out of my misery.

Standing in front of the mirror, I pulled a large section from the top, front of my head and whacked it off. The mirror reflected long hair hanging from my ears down my chest, while the hair on top of my head stuck straight up, two to three inches. I looked like the Crypt Keeper's creepy sister.

I felt a warped measure of success and grabbed more chunks of hair. I cut until the hair was between zero and two inches. I looked like I cut my hair in the dark with baby toenail clippers. It was awful and whimsical, in a crazy clown sort of way. *Eureka*! This was a disposable haircut!

I slowly sauntered by Brad and Emma in the den but no one noticed. I turned and made a second pass, slower still. I heard Emma say in her *oh no* voice, "*Mama.*"

Brad shook his head in disbelief and asked, "*What did you?*"

"I gave myself a *freakin' adorable* haircut. You don't like it?"

Two weeks after my first round of chemo, Brad and I met a group of my girlfriends for a movie, and then dessert.

I don't remember much about the movie and obviously I was distracted, because for over two hours, I gently plucked hair from all over my head. After the movie, our group gathered outside in the sunlight. I'd been at the rear of the group and when I entered the circle, everyone stopped talking and stared at me.

A compact mirror was immediately presented and the image made me want to laugh and cry. I'd plucked bald spots all over my head and I looked like I had the *mange*. I lightly pulled on a tuft and dropped it into the wind to show proof it'd come out voluntarily. After another pinch and more flying hair, we'd all swallowed the hard truth.

They wanted to be present for me, but no one knew what to do. My dear friend Pamela stepped forward and faced me. With her hands on my shoulders and in at a volume much louder than usual, she leaned forward and instructed, "*Feel your feelings. Feel your feelings!*"

I looked her in the eyes, thought about it, and reported, "I'm not hot, I'm not hungry, I'm not upset, and I'm not as freaked out as *you are*. Do you need to sit down?"

She was amusing in her honesty, "Yes I do. I really do. I need to sit down with a drink." I heard laughter and an offer to buy her a drink. Someone suggested P.F.Changs, and off we went.

That evening Brad shaved my head; no tears, no drama...*no more mange.*

Waiting for the shower, my happy thoughts are jolted when I hear a familiar voice, "Nope sorry, I'm next." I see Teresa walking toward me with her toiletries, but I inform her, "*Whatever*, I've already paid the lady."

She counters, "Maybe so, but I didn't *see* your name on the list. *I'm* next." I don't know what she's talking about. "What list? I didn't see a list. There isn't a list."

My confidence doesn't rattle her and she comes to rest in front of me. "Well, yes, there is a list, and you better go get your name on it." The shower door opens and Ruth emerges from perfumed steam.

Teresa boosts herself off the wall into the bathroom. Standing on the wrong side of the door I hear, "Man, it's hot in here, this feels good. Hey Bama, go get your name on the list!"

Teresa's strong, intelligent, attractive, successful, confident, bold, and maybe fearless. The bottom line—she's an amazing and beautiful badass, but if I knew how to cut off the hot water, I'd freeze her ass so hard right now.

I won't argue, but I won't go quietly either. I raise my voice through the crack of the door, "O.K., fine! How 'bout you enjoy that shower while I drag my crippled ass back upstairs!" Then I yell a quote from one of her favorite movies, Caddy Shack, "Thanks again for the worst looking hat I ever saw. I bet you got a free bowl of soup with it!"

When her laugh starts loud and long, I can tell it's is gonna be a good one. The intensity of her amusement gives me a temporary sense of satisfaction. The pleasant sensation lasts until

I get to the bottom of the stairs. I'm reminded, it was a temporary and hollow victory.

On the way up I complain to myself how the lady at the *bottom* of the stairs should have told me about the damn list at the *top* of the stairs. I remember she only said two words, and they were clear as day, "*You're next.*" I know going down is gonna hurt a lot worse than going up, and then I'll really want to thank Teresa.

When I reach the tearoom I see the lady behind the counter. I limp to her and beg, "Is there a *list* for the shower?"

She doesn't seem to understand, so I repeat myself, slower and louder. *"Is there a list ... for **the shower**?"* I jab both pointer fingers downward, in the direction of the bathroom. I stop and change hand motions to demonstrate water coming down and wiggle all my fingers furiously, directly over my head.

Her co-worker says something in Nepalese and reaches under the counter. He brings out an open notebook and places it in front of me.

At the top of the page is the word "Shower." I sigh. On the first line, there is indeed a signature. I groan. It plainly reads, "*Teresa.*"

Last morning at Imja Tse

Dr. Charlie returns the favor

In Tengboche with Mt. Everest on the left and on the right

Me with Mt. Everest and Michael

Kristin and Me waiting on lunch

Dr. Leah, Leslie and Me - Still waiting

# 26

## My Kingdom for a Horse Named Sweet Pea

*(Descent to Lukla–9,317 ft.)*

Our trek from Lukla to Namche took several days, but in reverse, we'll do it in just one. We've barely begun when the pain in my right knee becomes excruciating. I can no longer bend it, so I have to have enough room to make a half arc motion each step-down.

It takes a lot of extra time and I've already fallen behind. Being in the rear probably means I'll score Mary or John and as luck has it, I get both. I also score Leslie and co-strugglers Reverend Richard and "Hacking Carly" (I had nothing to do with that nickname but came to understand it).

I'm with the slowest of the slow and worried about our ability to make it to Lukla before dark. I've worked myself onto an anxiety ledge when I see an old rusty sign that reads "Horse can be found here." I throw an arm out and grab the jacket of the closest Sherpa and plead, "Is that for real? Is that a *real* sign? Can *I* find a horse here?"

He doesn't speak but nods yes. My odds are as bad as my options, and since I'm not sure he comprehends the seriousness, I grip his coat tighter. There's no room for fuzzy communication.

Anxiety amps my thoughts, "What if there are no horse rentals? What if this sign is old and useless? What if they only had two horses to start with, and they were *siblings?* They would have had square-headed babies and I'm fairly sure you can't ride a square-headed horse!"

I'll ride whatever is necessary to get to Lukla so I need to focus. My focused thoughts are as follows: Do people ride yaks? They obviously don't have sweeper vans here, but maybe I can get a ride on a sweeper yak.

I haven't seen anyone riding *anything* except for that medical helicopter. Well forget that. I'll live here before I get on a helicopter.

I put my face closer to the Sherpa and lower my voice, "Seriously dude, I *have* to have a horse. You don't wanna have to carry me down these mountains, but by George you will. *I need to see a man about a horse.*" He immediately recognizes both crazy and desperate and calls for a two-way radio.

"Please just get me a horse and get me to Lukla, O.K.? Thank you, *dhanyabad* so much." I straighten out his crinkled jacket and force a smile. I give him a look that validates his concern and admit, "I know dude; I'm losing it."

On the radio, the staff talk over each other in Nepalese, but I hear the same distinct word in English pinging throughout the conversation, "*Bama.*" Soon Lhakpa arrives and takes the radio. I'm positive everything will be O.K. He says another sentence in Nepalese and my Sherpa exclaims, "Yes! You have a horse!"

After the thought, "You speak English?" I cheer, "I knew you could do it! *Dhanyabad!*"

I have $80.00 on me, which is the exact cost of the horse. There are money machines in Lukla, so I can get more funds if I need to. I'll remortgage my house to pay for the ride if I have to.

I'm told I'll have to wait 45 minutes or so for the horse to be brought from a nearby village. We're on Sherpa time so I figure we're looking at hours, but I don't care. A different Sherpa is told to wait with me. I apologize that he has to wait, but he waves me off saying, "It's no problem, Bama."

"Thanks for being understanding, *Short Straw*." He looks at me funny and I explain, "That's what you drew to end up here with me."

He laughs and gives me a thumbs up, "No, *no problem* Bama."

I'm surprised that in less than 15 minutes, a horse arrives from a nearby village, freed up when a trekker decided he could walk again. I'm struck by a sense of false advertising from the sign. The animals on it are striking. This poor little fellow looks like a *hobbit horse.*

Let me describe this magnificent beast to you and warning—words fail. He's short, fat, and has bad teeth. Picture a crazy Bob Marley dreadlock colliding with a big Jerry Garcia curl and *bam*, his mane and tail are born. But I don't care because he's getting me out of here.

His handler is a pretty young Nepali female named Amentra. She has her long dark hair pulled into a ponytail and she tilts her head down when she smiles. She's the fourth and oldest version of the girl from my dream, so I instantly know and like her. I also realize this is the first female outside of a retail or lodge position I've seen in this country, and she's doing a *dude's* job. I dig that and I really want her to succeed.

I ask her, "What's your horse's name?"

"He doesn't have a name."

"That's silly because everybody knows his name is *Sweet Pea*."

She smiles and says, "O.K."

I saw them talking earlier so I know they're acquainted. I point, "Have you met Short Straw? My name is Suzanne."

He motions back at me, "No, this is *Bama*."

"I'm easy. You can call me whatever you'd like, as long as it's not late for dinner."

Early on, Sweet Pea shows a healthy sense of fear. When he balks on the first decline, Amentra tugs and pulls, but he won't budge. I wave her off, "I'll talk to him!"

I turn my attention to Sweet Pea and become the biggest cheerleader he's ever had. "O.K. Sweet Pea, I believe in you! You can do it! Come on now, Sweets. You gotta at least try." These mountain trails are hard and I don't know how old he is in dog years, but he's probably approaching triple digits.

Short Straw tells me the trails are often too steep even for a horse, much less one with a passenger. Furthermore, I'll have to dismount on the steeper inclines, the ones that cause pain in the first place. The new information is disturbing. I'm gonna have to take the pain, feel scared for my life, upset for causing suffering to an animal, and possibly guilty if a *girl* gets fired. What does a demotion look like?

As we arrive in Phakding, we pass A+BCers as they've finished lunch and are heading back to the main trail. I'm traveling down a long green lawn as pilgrims divide and make room. I feel kinda like Jesus going into Jerusalem, which makes Sweet Pea my donkey and I declare, "I love you donkey buddy!"

As I get closer to the tearoom, I'm giving it my best queen's wave. I hear Michael laughing his ass off and he yells, "Ala-freakin-Bama!"

I greet him and Andy who's taking a video with, "Whiskey for My Men and Beer for My Horses."

When I try to dismount my foot is caught in the stirrup and my knee won't bend. I have to lie at an odd angle on top of Sweet Pea. I hear Michael and Kristin having simultaneous attacks of "ILS."

"Hey, Michael and Kristin *I can hear you*. Which one of you is wheezing? I hope you both choke!"

They become riotous when Amentra finally frees my foot and I fall to the ground with a jarring thud. The pain feels like ice picks through both knees and profanities want to explode, but then I see *him*. It's the son of a bitchin' Walmart Greeter of the high Himalaya and he's headed straight to me. Even better, he's got his mother effin' arms outstretched for a soul-sucking hug. I don't want to see, hear, smell, or talk to *anyone*. It's nothing personal towards him, he's a victim of my severe pain's collateral damage.

I can only take a few steps before I have to bend over and clutch my knees. I congratulate my partner, "Yeah, Sweet Pea, we did it!"

Dr. Deming hugs me and asks, "What's your horse's name?"

Since he's not asking about me, I'm more tolerant and introduce him to my new best friend. "They said he didn't have a name but he does. It's Sweet Pea."

Kristin has stopped her wholly *Inappropriate Laughter* and calls out, "Hey, Suzanne, where's my Mom?"

Leslie was by my side until I got the horse. I figure she's in the rear with Mary and John, helping Carly and Reverend Richard.

With Michael, Andy, and Kristin back on the trail, I'm the sole trekker left in Phakding, besides Dr. Deming. I eat lunch quickly because I want to catch up with everyone.

When I'm finished I ask to speak with him outside over a Nettie pot. He's not in a hurry, so I take a cheap shot and issue a challenge, "Don't be a *scaredy pants*."

His chair slides on the hard floor and I know he's mobile.

Once outside we inhale warm salted water and exhale mud. When I'm done I offer to take his cup. He holds up a 'wait a second' finger and goes for round number three.

I tell him the real reason I wanted to see him and I'm emphatic, "Richard has got to get a horse, whether he wants to or not. John and Mary won't leave him, so innocent people will suffer. The Sherpa can take it, but Mary and John are mere humans."

I cut to the bottom line. "Look, some people just don't have enough sense to come in out of the rain, and Richard may be one of them. We *have* to tell him when it's time to come in out of the rain."

He assures me he'll take care of it as Reverend Richard and Carly enter the lawn, flanked by Mary and John. I'm ready to go, so after a quick bathroom break, I head out to find Sweet Pea and Amentra. Richard and Carly stand around a newly arrived horse.

Dr. Deming hurries over as I start to mount shouting, "Wait, Susannah Bama! The new horse is for Carly. Richard's is coming soon."

"Oh thank goodness. I'm relieved. Well, it's getting late and starting to rain, so ..." I start to mount Sweet Pea and *he stops me again*. What the hell dude?

He kindly requests, "Would you mind waiting? So you can all go together?"

"NO! Wait, why? Seriously, can't they just ...?" Each horse has a handler in front and a Sherpa behind so they don't *need* us to travel with them. I have a horse by right of consciousness and I want to keep moving and catch up with the group. I can't disguise my frustration and repeat, "Seriously, why?"

Deming says, "Lhakpa says it's safer for us to travel in a group."

"How long it will take for Richard's horse to get here?"

He seems uncomfortable, "Honestly, I'm not sure. They haven't found one yet."

"Aww, *come on man!*"

Lhakpa yells in our direction, "We'll have a horse here soon."

Wait. Are we talking *Sherpa soon*? I yell back, "How soon is soon according to the sun?"

Lhakpa laughs, "About an hour."

Now I want to know why we need to be so safe and ask, "So what are we looking at? Stagecoach robbers? Train bandits? Robin Hoods?" I have nothing left but a mustard seed of determination and a piss poor attitude.

Dr. Deming validates my feelings and I begrudgingly acquiesce, "O.K., fine, I'll do it. But *not* with a glad heart."

"Thank you, Susannah Bama." I look in his eyes and, I'm done. This man has asked nothing, yet given so much, I'm ashamed. "O.K., I'm sorry. I'll do it *with* a glad heart."

He thanks me but I take a final jab, "I'm ass-dragging tired so tell 'em to hurry every chance they get. It could get dark before we get there. At this rate, it could get dark before we *leave here!*"

I watch the doctor, along with John and Mary, walk back the way Sweet Pea and I entered. I look at Carly and Richard and roll my eyes. I yell after Deming one last time, "Thanks for abandoning me with the lady with pneumonia, and *especially* the one that likes to *mosey*. I'm really looking forward to *moseying* in the cold, dark, rain …in *full grown* mountains!"

Reverend Richard's laughing as he walks over and I continue, "I could've been half way to Lukla by now, but *noooooo*, I have to wait for the ones that have to be told to come in out of the rain!"

He hugs me and I thaw. I promised a glad heart, so after a bit of meditation, I adjust my attitude.

Sure enough within the hour, we're back on the trail: three busted-up trekkers, on three-busted up, or too small horselettes. Richard's horse is in the lead, therefore Richard's head is my focal point. Sweet Pea and I are in the last position and I understand that Amentra *can't* be in the lead.

I wonder if Amentra has older brothers to protect her. Do older brothers do that here, or are they mean and hateful?

My thoughts are interrupted when Short Straw yells at Sweet Pea. He may have swatted him with that stick thingy he's carrying, so I'm gonna pay attention.

The Sherpa for both Richard and Carly walk closely behind them, ready to steady or catch their rider. Short Straw's so far behind me, *he* may get lost.

I tease, "Look at them!" I point to the Sherpa tailing Richard and Carly. "But you. You're so far back, Sweet Pea and I could go ass over elbows off the side of this mountain, and you wouldn't know it for an hour."

He uses the stick thingy to shoo at me, "No. Two hours." I realize how much English Amentra knows when I hear her laugh.

It's been overcast most of the day and rain sneaks in after the heavy mist, causing the trail to become slippery. I yell, "Hey Richard, Check us out! We're a slippery demographic on a slippery slope. What kind of odds to you give us?" His response is loud, nervous laughter.

Everyone except for me puts on rain gear because I left mine in Kathmandu. Obviously abandoning weatherproof clothing to make the 30 pound duffle bag weight limit to Lukla was a mistake.

Richard puts on a *ginormous* blue poncho that covers him and his entire horse, except for its head, tail, and trembling hooves. It looks wrong *and* hysterical.

I yell at him, "Did you steal that tarp from the last village, or did you really use 20 of your 30 pounds transporting rain gear?

"It was this, or toilet paper."

"Richard, you crack me up! But I've used thousands of pounds of toilet paper, so I disagree with your call."

I'm watching this tall, large man on this teeny tiny horse. His long legs make it look like a "Flintstone Pony." The poor horse has almost capsized twice on steep inclines and flatly refuses to go down this next incline. The handler is taking it personally and a power struggle ensues.

When I see what Sweet Pea's up against, I initiate a dismount and yell at Richard, "Hey, dude, another slippery slope. How about getting off your high horse before you break it!"

I can tell he's nervous and since Sweet Pea's bigger than his horse, I should offer to switch. But I have too many of my own safety concerns and besides, Richard has a distinct advantage with the whole clergy gig.

I'm riding with my legs dangling outside the stirrups. The stirrups are too short and like my sleeping bag, youth-sized. I don't wanna freak out after making such a stink to get the damn horse in the first place, but I'd give away part of Dr. Deming's soul for a change in transportation modes.

My glad heart is being tested again, and now that I'm getting wet, I'm back to meditating.

We're consistently greeted by fresh faced trekkers wearing clean clothes. They greet us with huge smiles and their newly acquired salutation, *Namaste*. I'm in layers of dirty shirts, filthy khaki shorts over unwashed camouflage patterned long johns, and wearing a wool hat I bought in Namche. It's some sort of horse or giraffe in bright rainbow striped colors with black scraggly yarn down the center for a mane. Donning shades and greeting people with my now perfected queen's wave, people ask to take my picture atop Sweet Pea.

One of the groups wears matching shirts. I remember those days. The group's led by a couple of young fit men walking ahead of them, and chatting with *vigor*. I personally think they should save that energy for later, but they're exploding with questions. I limit my comments to, "Yes, the weather's been outstanding. (Pause) "Three Weeks.' (Pause) "*Namaste* to you, too."

I anticipate this group will have a similar level of pep, as their leaders, but I'm wrong. It's a silent, tired bunch, in all shapes, sizes, and ages, and they look like they've seen better days. Have mercy; they're a few hours out of Lukla and I'm *positive*, they're about to get their asses handed to them. With Batman and Robin for leaders, there could be fatalities.

I'm in the home stretch and I certainly don't want to piss on anyone's parade. But I've become a greater humanitarian and appeal to them, "It's not too late. You can turn around and go back with us. You don't *have* to follow them."

The last sentence causes enough laughter to stir the group's energy. I try to twist and face them as they pass, but I'm too stiff and swollen to turn. Instead, I do the best I can and tilt my head straight up as if about to howl, "Don't say you weren't warned!"

The loudest laughter belongs to Amentra. I poke fun with her, "You think it's funny because you *know* it's true. This time she laughs so hard she covers her mouth with her hand.

I reassure her, "That's O.K., we *all* thought it."

I know we're getting close to Lukla because the terrain is mostly straight up, and that's where Sweet Pea shines. He wants Amentra to go faster because everyone has a wheelhouse and he's in his. I recognize the backside of the sign that begins the trail out of Lukla. I remember it read, "Gateway of the Himalaya." The backside should read, "Welcome Back You Lucky Sons of Bitches."

I was the one who didn't want to come to Lukla in the first place, now I'm the very last one to return to her. I'm sure the whole group is already warm and cozy in the teahouse. They probably don't know we're MIA. It's close to 5:00 p.m. and because rain is sporadic, it's getting dark quicker than usual. I think it's Thursday, give or take a day.

When we arrive at our lodging in Lukla, I'm disturbed to hear that Amentra plans to take Sweet Pea back home tonight. How is that safe?

She dismisses my concern and I wonder how she learned to deal with her fears. Does she even have fears and if so, what are they?

I plead with her. "You can stay in the room with Ruth and me, and we'll hook Sweet Pea up too."

Again I'm politely dismissed as a kind and naïve, yet highly grateful, Bama.

I don't have any money left for a tip, so say, "Wait here, O.K.? Give me two minutes and I'll be right back. *O.K.?*"

I move as fast as I can to the tearoom. It sounds like they're watching sports because I hear cheering.

Sure enough, as soon as I walk in everyone erupts in more cheers and applause. I know it's for me because everyone is looking right at me, smiling and clapping. They really did miss us! These crazy kids are the best!

I wave but keep moving. I'm just looking for a quick loan and when a lender steps up, I head back outside with two ten-dollar bills.

Carly sees the money and stops me. "I need to tip my guy too. Can I have ten dollars?"

"I'm sorry, Carly, no. I had to borrow this for Amentra."

I hand Amentra the money, "I really appreciate your helping me today. I wish this were a lot more. Thank you so much for everything."

Both her smile and hug tell me she's happy to have been on the trail, too. Everything about her is genuine and warm, and I'm happy to have been able to spend several hours with her. She's amazing and I'll never forget her.

Sweet Pea swats a fly with his tail and I remind him how handsome he is. "Thank you, Sweet Pea. You're my bona fide hero."

He shakes his head and sprays spittle. I scratch his forehead hoping to curb another head shake. "I'm sure this wasn't your first choice either Buddha's belly, but you did a *perfect* job. You're short and fat, and I love you to pieces."

Amentra laughs and I shrug, "What am I gonna do? My white knight smells and has bad breath, but he's *load bearing*."

She can't contain her amusement and starts to cover the smile that can't contain the laughter. I intercept her hand, "Don't cover that smile. It's beautiful." She turns and leads Sweet Pea back the way we'd come.

They're going home, and wow, I'm going home too. I fling the first tear off my face before the second one bull-rushes out. My throat feels constricted so I don't try to swallow. If I exhale, I'll start bawling, so I hold my breath and watch Sweet Pea's broad backside recede into the mist. Someone calls my name.

It's Reverend Richard, "Hey Suzanne, *you need to come in out of the rain.*"

A similar sign

Riding in on Sweet Pea with Amentra and Shortstraw (one of the Tenzings)

Here comes the Walmart Greeter

# 27

## The Hardest Goodbye
### *(Leaving Lukla)*

The morning of October 8th I struggle to wake up and function. Flying out of Lukla will take three planes again, so the wake-up calls are staggered. I'm in group one, which means reporting to the tearoom at 4:30 a.m. I struggle and scramble, and finally yell out into the darkness and over the rail into blinding floodlights, to the Sherpas three floors below, "Somebody please tell them I'm coming, and y'all can get my bag whenever you want!"

They're in the courtyard, waiting on the yak. Maybe they're letting the poor beasts of burdens sleep in. I wonder, "How much sleep do yak need? Can they have sleep apnea? Do any animals have apnea? Marine life couldn't have it because they'd get water in their gills and choke to death. Wait a second, fish can't choke. I'll Google it later."

I'm having a hard time waking up even though I just had a decent night's sleep. I'm only four minutes late, but I'm banished to the second flight. I complain to Teresa, "Aww come on. Everyone's still here and all the luggage is too."

She says passenger information has been submitted and can't be changed back.

I'm curious and ask, "Who took my spot?"

She raises one eyebrow, then arches it into a question mark.

"Oh come on Teresa, I just want to *talk* to them. Who took my seat?" She remains tight lipped.

I flop on the closest bench and hear someone say, "Well, Bama, if you had to fly out based on where you placed in the race yesterday, you'd be on the last flight."

I sit up to see who said that shit but Teresa interrupts my investigation, "Yeah, Bama, you cost me money. I'd bet on you to win."

I hear echoes of "Me too," and "I bet on Bama."

Now I understand why everyone cheered when I walked into the tearoom yesterday. They'd been waiting for us by drinking beer and betting on the horses. I was favored to win, but came in third. Coming in last goes against my competitive nature so it's best I didn't know about the bet.

As they recount yesterday's horse race, it's clear to me they were betting on the *riders*, not the horses. I lie with my backpack for a pillow, eyes closed and listening to the excited activity around me. I recognize the voices of this group and feel soothed.

Comforted and warm, I fall *drool asleep* until someone calls my name and I have to wake up all over again. Maybe it's the extreme fatigue, but as I get in the van I can't shake the feeling I'm missing something. I'm oblivious to my surroundings during the drive to the airport, security, and ticketing. I blindly follow red-fleeced jackets until I remember how that turned out the last time. I'm extremely uncomfortable because, *I know I'm forgetting or missing something.*

I hate that feeling of missing out on things. Due to exhaustion I missed the ceremony last night after dinner when they gave Asian Trekking staff their cash bonuses, new or barely used crampons, and ice picks. And chef made apple pie. Ah geez I missed the apple pie. What am I missing *right now*?

As I approach the gate for "ticketed passengers only," it smacks me upside the head, "*Oh my god, I haven't said goodbye to Tenzing!*"

He went with the first group and I assume he's gone back now to get the third one. Well, they bumped me from one flight, so they can do it again! I'm frozen with nowhere to go until I figure out how to find Tenzing. The truth strikes me: "It may not be possible."

I'm about to burst into tears when I hear someone call my name. I turn towards my gate and *there's Tenzing!*

The relief on my face must be as obvious as the amusement on his. I run and hug him and blurt out my panic, "I didn't know if I could find you. I didn't know if I could say goodbye to you." I'm dehydrated but somehow liquid spills from my eyes.

Tenzing's almost laughing, "No, no, that wouldn't happen. It's good."

I continue babbling, "I don't know what to say, I don't know how to say it. You looked out for me, you helped me *so* much."

According to Ram Dass, "We're all just walking each other home" but I could never express enough gratitude for Tenzing's escort.

"Tenzing…wait a second. I don't even know your last name. And you were named for a day of the week!"

Now he's laughing out loud but he knows I'm *really* upset, so he counters with a slow and calm, "It's O.K., Suzanne. You can find me through (something uninterpretable)."

I have no idea what he's saying, but as usual, he's not worried, so neither am I.

While I don't know exactly how to say goodbye to Tenzing, I know exactly who I'm saying goodbye to. The man that made me feel safe, watched over, and protected. I want to meet his wife and children, family and friends, and learn more about his world. I want to meet the people who helped this man become the incredible person I now call my friend, my brother.

I'm so tired I feel dead inside, except that my chest hurts, and my throat is so tight I can't swallow. We've resumed our norm; I'm still crying and he's still giving me support. I hug him hard and long and as I walk away, I furiously warn myself, "This is the hardest goodbye in the world, so whatever you do, don't look back. Don't look back!"

When I look back, Tenzing's still smiling. But this time I know it's really good-bye, because this time, *his eyes don't smile back*

L-R Bikal, Me, Tenzing

L-R Andy, Michael, Tenzing, Dr. D

Our last night in Lukla, Tenzing far right

# 28

## Could Somebody Put a Bell on Me?
*(Lost in Kathmandu)*

After the first flight departs, a thick band of clouds descends and squats on the end of the runway. The clouds cause dangerous invisibility so transportation halts. Lukla's tiny airport has been shut down for several days due to weather, so a lot of trekkers are desperately trying to get in and out. Delays like this can last for days.

If that happens, I'll use the time to find out who was on the first flight and is already in Kathmandu at the Five Star Hotel. I want to know so I can ask them, "Who took your bribe and gave you my seat?" I'm after the *big* fish.

I fall asleep on Mary in the airport. She's been everywhere I've been, but somehow she's still upright, so that makes her my pillow. I move in and out of consciousness and eventually hear a horn followed by rumblings, "A flight from Kathmandu is in the air." That means that in 45 minutes the plane will arrive, and in 55 minutes we'll be airborne on it.

Like clockwork, in 45 minutes I go from dead asleep to boarding the plane that'll fly me out of the world's most dangerous airport. The adrenaline rush is insane. On the plane, Mary sits next to me and offers me the same rock she let me hold on our flight here, the one that says, "Hope." I decline it this time because being nervous requires energy. I have none of that.

The small plane revs and roars and lurches forward. We're hauling ass down the runway and I wonder why we haven't lifted off it yet. Out the window I see the plane's wheels weed-eating the grass *beyond* the runway. My eyes get big and my jaw drops and Mary grabs my hand. The plane drops off the end of the strip and I'm on a roller coaster, free-falling and weightless. The plane drops for mere seconds until it begins to rise and soar. When I'm rhythmically synched back into my body and seat, I pat Mary's hand emphatically and reassure her, "You're O.K. You're O.K."

She holds my hand until we're over the first mountain. I like helping Mary.

I struggle desperately to stay awake as the Himalayan Mountains peek above the clouds. I'm too fuzzy-headed to imagine the awesomeness beyond them and fall asleep so many times that by the time I get to the room in Kathmandu, the lines of reality are blurred.

Ruth's waking up from a nap and getting ready to shower by the time I arrive. I walk to the unruffled bed and face plant. For the next three hours, I sleep hard and when I awake, I'm groggy and hungry.

After a quick shower, I head to the courtyard restaurant for a late lunch. It's Friday, October 12th, and the weather is beautiful. This last day on the other side of the world is turning out to be perfect. Kim and Marilyn invite me to sit with them and I'm struck by how fantastic and well-rested they look. Fortunately, they were released from the hospital the same day they were medevac'd in.

They've spent the last week getting to know the real Kathmandu and having an amazing time exploring and learning. After making a few trips to a local boy's school – The Regina Amoris School – they've started a charity to raise money for these underprivileged children.

Michael allowed me to use his phone in Phakding to text Brad and get my debit card reinstated. I hope it worked since I'm completely out of money. Marilyn and Kim know their way around and offer to escort me to the nearby ATM. Marilyn adopted a street cow that's always within a few blocks of the hotel and wants to make her daily visit to see it.

At the ATM, I get $100 dollars to last me until I get home. I'll be on an airplane for the majority of that time, so I'm sure $100 is enough. I put the money and debit card in one pocket and check to make sure the small brass room key is still in the other.

Marilyn offers to walk me back to the hotel but I say, "Don't be silly. I'll go two blocks that way, make a right at your cow, then it's another few blocks down on the left. It's not like I can get lost again and again, and sigh, again. I'm not going for a hat trick in getting lost."

Marilyn and Kim are going to dinner tonight with some local friends they've made, so they'll miss A+BC's farewell dinner. I wish them a pleasant evening and tell them I'll see them in the morning. We part ways and I head to the cow.

It's a busy Friday afternoon full of people and traffic. I'm lily-white, freckled, and not wearing a hat, so I stand out like a bleach stain on a dark sweater.

After about ten minutes of fumes, dust, and stares, I think I should have reached the hotel. I wish I'd let Marilyn guide me back. She's practically a native by now.

I look for some sort of civil service uniform to approach and finally see a young guy directing traffic in a busy intersection. He's the stop sign, the red light, and the green light. He has to focus.

I wait on the flow of traffic to ease up, or for him to somehow acknowledge me, and hopefully communicate something to the effect of, "I see you lost and afraid tourist. I'll be with you soon to assist you to safety." After several more minutes without any deviation from his routine, I know he won't be assisting me.

I continue walking because I couldn't have missed an entire, *inordinately huge* hotel. Then it hits me like an *inordinately huge* hotel, I've missed it

I need a place to cross the street and retrace my steps, but the roads have widened, while the walking spaces have shrunken. I stay to the right to try and wind through less traveled backstreets. I think I'm getting back on track until I come to yet another unfamiliar intersection. Now I'm positive I'm lost. I remember thinking the first night we wound through the dark streets on our way to dinner that only an idiot or a fool would allow themselves to get lost here. Now it's official; I'm an idiot *and* a fool.

Maybe I can say the name of my hotel to a stranger, hold my palms upward, and shrug my shoulders. Then it dawns on me, "Oh my god! I don't know the name of my hotel! I don't know the freaking name of my freaking hotel! It starts with an M, maybe Masala? No, that's an Indian spice.

I can't believe I don't know the name of my bastard hotel, but in my own defense, I never planned on getting lost. This repeat performance is extraordinarily unnerving. I'd never be afraid to be lost in Times Square or any part of the U.S. I probably wouldn't be afraid to get lost in any part of the world that has a sewage system.

Maybe the kidnappers will be kind enough to tell me the name of the *freaking* hotel if we pass by it.

Where's Tenzing? Where's Radar or Short-Straw? I really need a Sherpa right about now. I want to call 911 but I don't have a phone and I doubt they have that service here anyway. I imagine the conversation with the 911 operator:

OPERATOR: "*Namaste*. Do you need police, ambulance or fire? *Just kidding*, we don't have any of those."

ME: "No, I'm fine, thank you. But I'm lost somewhere here in Kathmandu. I'm staying at a hotel that starts with an M and reminds me of a curry. Can you help me find it? Dhanyabad *so* much."

I can't find anyone who speaks English and every time I ask, I feel more like a fish in a bowl. Then it hits me—I am the alien here. I'm the foreigner so why shouldn't they look at me like that?

I need to keep moving so I decide to retrace my steps on a less busy street. Streets in a well-planned city should be approximately parallel at consistent distances, but these blocks aren't even close. I'm suddenly at a new intersection that's the hub of half a dozen streets.

It looks like a dirty, old and unlit New York Times Square. All the buildings are five to eight stories tall and connected. They aren't level or straight, so the streets pass by them at odd angles. The construction appears distorted and creates optical illusions.

I have to stay focused and calm because I feel *completely* disoriented and overwhelmed.

Nothing is familiar and in fact, the environment is somehow pricklier. It suddenly hits me. No one even knows I'm lost. The last ones to see me were Kim and Marilyn, and they aren't going to the restaurant tonight. I may not be missed until bedtime and that's waaayy after dark!

I'm processing a lot of scary stuff at once. I'm lost in a huge city in a third world country, and I'm so far away from home, I'm in a different day. I'm experiencing exhaustion that borders on collapsing. I'm mentally and emotionally spent.

This list of how many ways I'm screwed should be paralyzing me with fear, but for some reason, it doesn't. I'm right in the middle of a huge rogue wave of *not good*, but I'm determined to ride it to shore. Extreme struggles lead to extreme insights, and I'm becoming a *master* at extreme.

At this point, Janis or Alice would normally react, but nothing within me stirs. I can't muster a sarcastic thought, and I'm too stunned to cry. Alice has become a Buddhist and accepts the suffering. Janis has no need to react.

I know these parts of myself well and sometimes they get in the way. I'm often my own worst enemy… too sensitive or too aggressive, too silly or too serious, too intense or too relaxed, always too much of this and not enough of that. But now I'm confident, my screwed up Gestalt is greater than the sum of my weird-ass parts.

I learned my elder's expectations and tried to shape my personality accordingly. The margins of error were narrow and coloring outside the lines was unacceptable. In my attempts to shrink, bend, and mold myself, I often felt inadequate and defective. I didn't know certain truths about myself and as a result, I never discovered my own *true North*. Now, I'm learning to trust and respect myself at new levels. I don't have to crumble, or go Rambo. I simply have to *trust life*.

This trip has been Pentecostal in nature, a constant Baptism of challenges and triumphs, pain and ecstasy, and above all, love and growth. I've proven to myself that I'm not just strong, I am indeed, *"strong like bull."*

I look up at the sky and it's beautiful. It's the same sky the Sherpa are under. It's the same sky Emma and Brad are under. I flash on a map of galaxies and see the dot, "You are here." This small, perfect world is *un-freaking-believable*. I petition the Universe, "Please tell me what to do, show me, and stay *very* close to me. Also, I don't think this is funny."

Standing in the middle of peaceful chaos, I go to what I know and breathe slower. When I stand up again, I'm straighter. The buildings are standing straighter too. Traffic may be slower, and I swear, I have elbow room.

I know what to do. I need to stay in a public place, but move away from this intersection. I have to somehow spin backwards into a different direction, on these busy streets. I see a bicycle-rickshaw and I'm inspired. I decide I can tail it across this intersection. About half way it occurs to me I might be in his blind spot, so he might turn and crash into me.

We're almost to the other side and I've accelerated as fast as my jacked-up knees will let me. I'm yelling at the rickshaw driver, "On your left. On your left!" but he doesn't seem to hear me.

I'm running as fast as I can but I can't catch him. He's peddling his ass off to get a load of passengers safely through this mess. And now he has this crazy foreigner racing him?

I don't slow down until I reach a side street and by then, I'm spent.

The first retail store I come to is women's clothing. A young guy with long brown hair leans in the doorway, watching me with casual interest. I look at him and he smiles. I look harder into the windows of his soul and he dips his head a bit to show he's looking back. I enter his store and take sanctuary.

The inside is small, cramped, and hot. But the lanky clerk is friendly and speaks some English. His face is Nepalese, but his hair color is lighter. He's probably a hippy. How wonderful for him. His racks of clothes are interesting and artistic, but they're covered in dust. Does anyone, ever, try them on? How does this wonderful hippy make a living?

I collect a heavy armload of clothing and ask for the dressing room. It's nothing more than a corner nook, with fabric strung over a rope for a makeshift curtain. There's nowhere to put my stuff, so as I disrobe, everything hits the floor where I stand.

The shop's only mirror leans against the checkout counter so I get to chat with the clerk often. I'm surprised when clothes don't fit. I seem to be at a higher "holiday weight" even though I've spent the last three weeks doing high-as-hell level cardio. Forget the fact that for days I didn't eat enough to keep a bird alive. But looking in the mirror, I notice I have *giant man hands* and my fingers are *huge*. Wait, I gained weight in my fingers? I struggle to put my toe shoes back on (the kind with individual sleeves for each toe), because my feet and ankles are bigger too.

I remember looking in a mirror in Namche and being concerned. At over 15,000 ft. high my face reacted like a baked potato left too long in a microwave; it became grotesquely swollen. But I'm back at sea level so why am I still functioning as a water tower?

Almost an hour passes by the time I'm ready to leave, and I spend $70 of the $100 I just took out of the ATM. This guy has been so kind he deserves a good payday and he seems grateful for it. I'll go back to the ATM before we leave tomorrow, no biggie.

My new friend steps outside and asks a retail neighbor if he knows of my hotel. He says he *thinks* he does, but even if he's right, he can't tell me how to get there because it's 20 minutes away through a crooked maze. This situation has all the makings for a bad ending, but since the sun is getting lower, I have to take action, even if it's the wrong one.

I've barely gone half a block when a man walks up to me out of nowhere and asks where I'm going. He's neatly dressed in gray slacks and a white long-sleeve dress shirt marked with small gray pinstripes. He looks to be in his mid-fifties and he seems nice enough. I figure there's no harm in getting his opinion and when he says the name of my hotel, I'm ecstatic! Then he tells me a similar version of how it's impossible to explain how to get there, but for two dollars, he'll take me.

I look around and don't see any cars or taxis. I think, "Go away, creepy American tourist serial-killer." It's like a bad Lifetime B-movie where you want to stop watching but you can't. You've invested just enough in the main character, you want to see how she dies. I look back at the man and tell him sternly, "No thank you, I'm good."

He understands my tone and reacts quickly, "No, no, in a taxi. I have a taxi. Here, I'll show you." He holds his arm out to usher me toward a side street but I counter his arm with my own, "I don't think so."

Again he gets it and immediately bows his head and drops his arm, "No, sorry." Now he points and when I follow his finger, I see a row of empty white cars with no lights on top, and no writing on the sides. "You should let me take you. It's too confusing and you'll get lost."

I point out the obvious, "I'm already lost."

He's paternal when he responds, "Not at night. No, is not good at night." I've heard that before, right Martha?

There's a young couple standing nearby watching us and I look to them. The guy says to me, "Is O.K., he is taxi." I look at the girl and she puts her hands together and says *Namaste.* She looks at the man in the gray slacks, then back to me and nods her head indicating approval. She holds my gaze and I sense it's alright to go with him.

I resign and get in the back of his small, white, nondescript car, void of any identification on the dashboard. As he drives he asks where I'm from and when I tell him the story, he's very interested. He's lost people to cancer and thinks the idea of a group of cancer survivors trekking the high Himalaya is fantastic.

Traffic is congested and slow and we make frequent turns. A long time passes before I begin to recognize anything and then he assures me, "Yes, is two more left turns." If I've learned one thing about Kathmandu traffic, it's that left-hand turns are the worst. They can be slow and treacherous at the same time.

Waiting at a standstill gives me a chance to purvey street vendor wares. When I see the t-shirt I've been looking for since my first day in Nepal I inform my driver, "That's the one. I want that t-shirt. I'll just get out here and you won't have to make the left turns." I start taking money out of my short's pocket, but he quickly protests, "No, is not so safe. You have a group right? Come back with your group O.K.?"

I think I'm doing him a favor by saving him some time, but he's not interested. I'm not sure why, but I completely trust his intentions. My sense of direction in Nepal is obviously impaired, so perhaps, is my judgement. I may be projecting Tenzing onto this man, but I agree and stay in the cab.

Ten minutes pass before we're able to approach the left-hand turn. This turn will takes us through a gate. The gate is always manually operated, and isn't left open after passages. The gate is attached to a 15' tall fence that surrounds the entire hotel compound. It's implemented tastefully and organically so, you'd have to be 16' tall to see over it.

I'm not surprised I couldn't find it. I'm just surprised anyone could.

I continue untangling money from my pocket and when I'm empty, I think it adds up to about $10. When he pulls up to the front door, I hand it to him and say, "Dhanyabad, *so, so,* much."

His entire face lights up and he folds his hands, and bows his head, "*Namaste.*"

As I enter the hotel, I see a few early birds gathered in the lobby. They have a clear view of me making closure with my taxi driver. Jeff, the protective oak, says, "Bama, it's getting dark." He points at the taxi, "Do you really think *that's* a good idea?"

I start laughing, "No, no I don't. I probably won't do it again."

Reverend Richard reminds me we have to meet in the lobby in less than an hour for dinner, and I know I have to hurry. I head to the fourth and top floor. When I take the key out of my pocket I pat another one to feel my debit card, but the pocket's empty. I start slapping myself all over trying to connect with a plastic rectangle, but all my pockets are empty. I shake the retail bag upside down and send my new purchases flying all over the hall. Twenty dollars is the only thing in the bag besides the clothes. Give me a break! I've lost my debit card somewhere between the shop and the taxi, so it may as well be on Mars. I have to call Brad so he can cancel the card *stat*.

I go to the front desk where I'm taken to an adjoining small room and an operator calls Brad. It's 5:20 a.m. in Charlotte and it's a long shot the phone will wake him. When he answers, I greet him, "Hey Hon, can you hear me?" His gasp is absurdly loud so I ask, "Wow, you're *really* surprised. Am I rumored to be dead?" I finish the call in under three minutes and pay the operator $12.

I hurry through the lobby and as I jog past Teresa she cautions, "Slow down Bama. It's not a race."

I defend myself, "As if *you'd* tell me if it was? You've lost *all* credibility lady!" I'm hobbling for my life when I hear the beginning of her laugh, and feel satisfaction.

I call the concierge to borrow a hair dryer. Turns out, the one they have is on loan to the room directly across from mine. They can't tell me the occupants' names, but I bet they're A+BC folk. I tip-toe across the hall and lean in close to the door, and listen in.

The TV in that room is playing the same movie as mine, Top Gun, 1986. The laughter inside tells me these are people I know; it's Leslie and Kristin.

I borrow the hair dryer and a short time later, Kristin knocks on my door and calls, "Hey Bama?" I figure they need the hair-dryer back but when I open the door, Kristin is standing with her arm extended, and her hand made into a fist. I reach out and she drops a blue bead into my palm. It's one of the beads we shopped for the first day in Kathmandu. I remember several shared experience with them; the Nettie pot with Kristin, and helping them untangle their prayer flags.

I remember how they helped me last night in Lukla. After I was told that the owner of a nearby deli might give me some cash on my card for a small fee, they volunteered to go with me. I didn't get any money, but Kristin and I discovered an empty night club in the basement of the deli. While colored disco lights swirled, Kristin and I danced to an 80's song. I just met these people two weeks ago and already, I love them so much.

Leslie pops her head into the room and asks if I'm ready to go. We head to the lobby together but part ways when I have to choose the elevator. My knees are much better, but stairs are still unreasonably painful. Leslie and Kristin head for the stairs.

Stepping into the elevator I issue the challenge, "Last one down is a dirty rotten egg!" I hear the pounding of feet on stairs and as the door closes and I holler, "See ya suckas!"

I know these elevators are so antiquated they may still operate on a weight and pulley system. I hear Leslie and Kristin flying down the stairs shouting encouragement to each other.

I can tell they're keeping pace with the elevator and as we get close to the second floor I rant loudly, "Y'all better slow down and be careful because this is how people get hurt!"

Kristin yells, "Hurry Mom!"

As soon as the elevator hits the lobby I start beating the "open door" button. I hear them stomping down the last flight of stairs until there's only one set of shoes.

Come on door! "Hey y'all, I'm already here!" I'm wedging myself through the crack as Leslie's hits the bottom step. Kristin's already in the lobby and Leslie and I are an equal distance from her. We make eye contact, and a tie is declared.

But rightfully so, Kristin *owns* her victory. I try to short-change her celebration by, "Well, it's not like there's a "Queen of the Masala Hotel."

Leslie corrects me, "Bama, it's *The Hotel Malla*." I chide myself aloud, "Good *gawd* Suzanne, it's **Malla**. It's **The Hotel Malla**."

Yeah, I'm not sure I'll remember the name, but *I'll never forget the experience.*

Marilyn and Kim

Marilyn's Cow

# A Random Buzzard In Kathmandu

Lost in Kathmandu

Lost in Kathmandu

L-R Mary, John, Me, Rev. Richard, and Dr. Leah

# 29

## The Stank of Sausage Feet and Home Sweet Home

I'm on my last leg, literally *and* figuratively, but *I'm almost home.*

We've retraced our flights back through India and into Amsterdam. The whole scene is kind of an ugly *déjà vu*. The last time we landed here, ambulances waited on the tarmac to take the man with the stroke to the hospital. Now they're waiting to take one of us. The *un*Zen is taken by a waiting ambulance to Amsterdam University Hospital.

We've been cleared to head to US soil. Our group is an early arrival at the gate so most of us have seats. The other passengers begin to fill in spaces around us and a guy, mid-twenties wearing a Michigan sweatshirt catches my eye; I get caught up on three weeks of college football scores. Alabama is still undefeated. (SPOILER ALERT – They beat LSU 21-0 to claim the 2012 National Championship! The THIRD National Championship in FOUR years!)

Kelly overhears me telling the guy how my *ex-best friend* Martha and her husband Phil, graduated from Michigan. The words "Hail to the Victors valiant…" spill out of her alumni mouth and because I've sung the fight song so many times I'm programmed and join in, "…Hail to the conquering heroes…"Michigan sweatshirt chimes in, "Hail! Hail! to Michigan, the champions of the west!"

I just sang a fight song that isn't "Yea Alabama" but it was a college fight song so it's thrilling. I'm so happy until Dr. Deming returns from the hospital and stands directly behind my chair. He shares the *un*Zen's medical status, "She's in the ICU, but she's stable."

I can't believe it. She's crazy fit except for whatever attacked her on this trip. It's probably intestinal, but with all the yak dust we've inhaled, bronchial infection is a reasonable diagnosis. Severe dehydration and malnutrition are also logical choices. Shut up brain and listen to him!

He continues, "She been diagnosed with a reform of a dull on cottage cheese."

With what? Did he say, *"A hair from adult set of beat ease?"* My ears are still stopped up so I turn around to read his lips and ask, "What did you say?"

He repeats, "She's been diagnosed with *a rare form of Adult Onset Diabetes*. Her son is flying in as soon as possible. She's in great hands."

A rare form of adult onset diabetes? A RARE FORM OF ADULT ONSET DIABETES! *No stinkin' way!*

She's been verbal in her opinions about certain trekkers and their situations, but she's spoken from a place of knowledge and experience. She was terse as hell, but this seems like extreme Karmic weigh-in. Or maybe, it's just one giant, weird-ass, coincidence. I'm afraid for her and pray for her immediate healing. This is another one of those "what the hell?" moments I'll have to process later, but the flight is announced and it's time to board.

I don't remember the flight across the pond, but I'm 100% aware when we land in Detroit, USA! It's mid-afternoon and the sky is blue and the sun is shining.

I'm glad my gate is on the same concourse as the one to Iowa. I get to spend a few more minutes of this odyssey, with these people. I never planned on new friends at this level. I never planned on the level of suffering it would take to forge these bonds, BUT, *I wouldn't change a single thing.*

Kelly yells, "Hey Bama! I think they changed your gate. And it's on a different concourse!"

I double check then thank her, "Of course they did, and of course, it is."

I have to go to the opposite side of the airport but I don't mind. Distance is now and forever more irrelevant.

Once at my gate, I gravitate close to the jet way. I'm afraid I won't hear the announcement and I'll miss my flight, so I write a note on a leftover Burger King napkin, and set it on top of the *hostess* stand. "Please don't let me sleep through the Charlotte boarding. I'm going home!"

My backpack is a large and entirely uncomfortable pillow; it's completely sufficient. Hello Kitty is stuck on *repeat*, so Michael Buble pulls me deeply into his ballad, *Home*.

> Another summer day
> has come and gone away
> in Paris and Rome,
> but I want to go home.
> May be surrounded by, a million people I,
> still feel all alone, just wanna go home.
> Oh, I miss you, you know?"

I drift in and out of sleep as this song plays again and again.

> "Let me go home
> I'm just too far
> from where you are
> I wanna go home."

I hear my flight number and jolt; a complete overreaction based on excessive adrenaline. The boarding process is painfully slow so I lean against the jet way wall. Buble incites me:

> "And I feel just like
> I'm living someone else's life.
> It's like I just stepped outside
> when everything was going right."

I stow my bag in the overhead and slide into my window seat. A man takes the aisle seat as I cram my backpack under the seat in front of me. A young professional woman in her late twenties claims the middle seat. She's consciously dressed to impress and has an expensive floral aroma that's subtle and elegant. My guess is high-end medical sales but I don't care: I want to inhale her.

After adjusting my seat belt, I can tell I have lost *a lot* of weight, regardless of what my phalanges suggest. I extend my arms to better examine my circus clown hands and utter aloud, "Dang. This can't be right."

My seatmate takes an interest and I find out that she's getting her Ph.D. in something to do bioscience, or agriculture engineering; something impressive and cool. Her name is Donna and she's headed to Atlanta for the weekend for a symposium on said field. She admits she's not an expert on the subject, but she's pretty sure, "You probably won't die from fat hands before we land, *probably*."

Hahaha and rah, the young clean smelling professional has a sense of humor.

She's highly intelligent and educated, and when she smiles, her teeth are perfect and brilliant. I look forward to brushing my teeth thoroughly.

She continues talking, "Its *fat feet* you have to worry about. Fat feet mean swollen ankles, swollen ankles mean swollen legs. When it gets to the legs, that's when it's bad. That's when strokes happen." I've heard people smell toast when they're having a stroke. I don't want to smell toast, and I don't want to talk to Donna anymore.

When the captain turns off the "fasten seatbelt sign," I get comfier and commit a sin of enormous proportions, in a most grievous manner. I take off my shoes. But not just any shoes. I take off my "toe shoes" (each toe has its own individual sleeve and yes, they are very comfortable). I've been wearing them non-stop for two days and when I peel them off, fluid filled feet explode into freedom. It's like nicking a Jimmy Dean sausage wrapper and the sausage explodes three times its original size. The wrapper then becomes useless.

I'm probably retaining fluid from several locations throughout the Himalayas, but fluid retention isn't the presenting problem. That would be the *foot odor from hell*. I'm equal measures of impressed and mortified by the smell. I hope it's not as bad as I think when a *loud* female voice in the row behind me exclaims, "Oh my god, what's that smell?!"

The man in the seat beside her offers, "Maybe there's a baby on board."

Even though she's behind me, she's in the aisle seat and I'm at the window, so I can see her when I turn around. She's petite and fastidious. She's wearing small-framed glasses and she's stunned her coif immobile with varnish; there will be no stragglers. The barrette is superfluous, but remains close by at her temple...just in case. She's also wearing her winter coat inside a cabin that has to be 75 degrees.

She's adamant about the smell, "No, *no*! It's worse than that!"

I shove the shoes under my backpack and smush everything forward as far as I can. I want to be done the drama, but I hear a nasally, high-pitched voice making FBI reports to everyone around her. I can't think in complete sentences anymore, much less try to explain and apologize for offending her delicate faculties. I simply *can't*.

She reminds me of Justin when he was stuck on, "Hey, Suzanne, say something hillbilly." I want to tell her *exactly* what I told him, but *this time*, I'd mean it.

I have to put my shoes back on and I gotta do it *fast*. Nancy Drew will figure out where the smell is coming from, and if she finds out how long I've worn the shoes and where they've been, she may lose her mind.

I slide down in my seat and extend my legs to pin and drag the offenders back. When I try to slip them back on I get a rude awakening. *My feet are enormous* and they're *not* going back in the shoes. After a few more attempts with brute force, I have to settle on damage control. I rest my Hobbit-sized feet on top of the shoe's attempting to stifle the smell.

I sit upright to re-fasten my seatbelt, but after readjusting my jacket, I'm hit with it again. *Aww, come on, man,* stink's on my *fingers!* What was an offensive smell to this woman has now escalated into a vulgar assault. She barks at the man beside her, "Do you smell it *now?!*"

The flight attendant distracts me with an offer of pretzels that I want, and water that I need, but I can't extend my stinky hands across two innocents. Instead, I pull my seat-back tray down, look at her, then back to the spot she should put my snacks. She holds out her hand a little bit further, but she isn't going to rudely lean over two passengers for no apparent reason. *Think, Suzanne, think.*

And then, as the Grinch would say, "I have a wonderful awful idea." *I'll be the rude one.*

I pull my jacket sleeves down over my hands and hold my fabric covered palms out. Tilting her head, she hands me the pretzels, then places the bottle of water directly on my tray.

The woman behind me will *not* let it go and I catch her seat mate's newest placation, "Maybe someone's got air sickness."

She cuts him off, "*No!* I know what *that* smells like, but this …"

I need to distract her, so I turn around while shaking my head vigorously and commiserate, "I know, right? I get a lil' whiff of something every now and then *too.*" I don't make eye contact though, because like people rank drugs, I rank sins. I might lie for a good enough reason, but I'm not gonna be a hypocrite. That's flat out *bad character.*

As I turn back around, I see Donna's profile. She's suppressing laughter, so I know she knows. Thankfully, she has a sense of humor, *and compassion.*

I replace my earbuds. The "repeat" function is still stuck on Hello Kitty but I've accidentally been able to change songs. When the MP3 lights up again, I hear Adele singing, "Make You Feel My Love." Her voice is strong and seductive, and it soothes me,

> "When the rain is blowing in your face
> and the whole world is on your case,
> I could offer you a warm embrace,
> to make you feel my love."

For the next hour, I rest my head against the window while absently observing the landscape far below. I play scenes in my mind from the past three incredible weeks as Adele tells me on repeat, over and over and over, what she would do to make me feel her love.

My brain is trying to synthesize three weeks at once as my heart overflows with love and gratitude. I'm not going to allow myself to cry, *yet*, but I get toilet paper out of my backpack, just in case. I also take out my yellow prayer flag and see it as if for the first time. I see the plane, the heart, and read the words, "Dear God, Thank you for embracing these souls. I pray you grant peace to all that loved them. Amen."

The worst thing I feared happening to me, happened to someone else. I could've died flying into the world's most dangerous airport, but the crash was delayed for two days. I could have died with cancer, or acute altitude sickness, from getting lost, or from an angry monkey.

But I'm still here, so do I ask, "Why *them*, and why not *me*?" The question feels pointless, so maybe the question is much bigger.

Is there a God, and if so, how much participation is involved?

If not, is life a sequence of random events we can only influence through our choices?

**God, or, coincidence?**

As time creates distance, the obvious becomes obvious – the truth is the same no matter which side of the fence you're on. "*If you believe it's **God**, then it's "His or Her will." If you believe it's random chance (better known as **coincidence**), then it's "bad luck.*"

Giving credit or blame for *why* or *why not* something happens is a waste of time. Yeah, it could have been my plane that went down – but for the Grace of God, (or the bad sense of direction of a random buzzard) there go I."

Insight eliminates needling over details. Gratitude is treated like a *verb*. It doesn't matter who or what I attribute events to. I'm not guaranteed today, and tomorrow often seems like a long shot. Every day is a gift for which I have no entitlement or assurance. What I have is *right now* and the freedom to think, feel, and choose in *this* moment.

If it was God's will, then I still have work to do and I need to get on it. If it was random chance, then I still have work to do and I need to get on it.

I get to dance, and I'm dancing for the 19 souls that had to turn in their dancing shoes too early, on the morning of September 28, 2012.

I'm dancing for all the souls gone due to cancer. I'm humbled by the privilege. Change that last sentence to, "I'm humbled by the privilege, and respectful of the *responsibility*."

When the Captain announces we're 20 minutes from Charlotte, the sun is parting ways with another Carolina blue sky. I know these clouds are North Carolina clouds. Why do they look so different from the ones on the other side of the world? It can't be the angle. I was looking *down* on the clouds in Nepal; I was also *standing*.

I want to freeze time to make sure I get everything in order. I'm afraid that breaking through the clouds will break this dream. Surely that's what the past three weeks have been.

A few times, the dream felt somewhat like a nightmare, but those parts will end up as some of the richest colors in this tapestry. The world I've just experienced is so different from my own, I'm afraid the two can't coexist. This trip to Nepal is the hardest and most rewarding thing I've done in my life. My gratitude is inexhaustible.

I remember the dream I had at Martha's before the trip –

"I'm in a dimly lit space that feels like a Vaudevillian theatre, except there's no seating. Velvet burgundy curtains form the walls and the stage is empty. I'm surrounded by people, but don't feel crowded by them. I wonder what we're all waiting for and it hits me, I'm expecting someone to roll a mirror onto the stage. Not a reflecting glass, or a fun-house image distorting one. *This mirror is going to let me see myself through the eyes of others, maybe these strangers.*"

The challenges of this trip caused everyone to stand naked before the Buddha. These people got to know me at my best *and* worst, *crusty boogers and all*. I feel love and acceptance from this group of people I've just met, and now, I instinctively call them *family*.

Speaking of family, I can't wait to see Brad and Emma. I've missed them fiercely, but I made a conscious decision when I left Charlotte to limit my thoughts about them to daily prayers. Flat on my back and in a hell of a battle with altitude sickness at base camp, I had to cut them out completely.

I left home with my big girl panties on and when a man had a stroke somewhere in the middle of the Atlantic Ocean, I suited up. I put on every big girl thing I owned: brass knuckles, steel-toed boots, chaps and choke collar. Now I'm sure my appearance is laughable. I stink and I'm skunk dead tired. But it's all good because *I'm almost home.*

My mind gives me a green flag when the plane breaks through the clouds. The familiarity of the Carolina landscape catches my breath: rolling hills washed in fall colors of red, yellow, and orange. Following instructions for landing, Adele becomes silent.

On the tarmac, the captain informs us of an eight to ten-minute delay to the gate and the cabin emits a collective groan. I make good use of the time by trying to get mammoth feet into marble sacks. It's not happening, no way, no how, so I wrap the airline blanket around my shoes in it as tightly as possible, but since there's no space in my backpack, I have to stow them inside my jacket. I'm careful to zip the jacket to the top to muffle residual smell.

Now I look ridiculous *and* suspicious; Donna is in full blown muffled laugh. I ply her, "What if the flight attendant thinks I'm trying to *steal* a blanket, and hide it in my coat? *You* carry my shoes off the plane. You're like a free-hall-pass." She laughs so hard she snorts. I egg her on, "Hey I'm curious, what size shoe do you wear?" Her snort draws more attention. I go silent.

I deplane barefoot and head to the nearest ladies room to *shoe-up*. My gate is at the tip end of the terminal. How far can it really be? My perception of distance has been permanently reconfigured.

However, riding on an escalator with dangling appendages, that's just *asking* for trouble. The wrestling match between foot and shoe has begun in earnest when I hear huffing and puffing at the sink above me. I'm bent over so I only see the shoes and the pants. Her *grunt-snorts* are about to turn into words and I freeze when I hear the craggily whine, "This is what I call a bad day, and I know bad days. Thank goodness that flight's over. The turbulence was awful!"

It's the back seat bloodhound and I can only pray

She doesn't recognize me. I address the hem of her pants, "My flight wasn't turbulent. You're talking about the one from Detroit?"

"*Yes, Detroit!* You sat in the row in front of me!"

Yep, she recognizes me and she's *definitely not* in a good headspace.

*If she smells my feet again, she'll know it was me all along.* We'll end up on the evening news for sure. I need to get out of here.

I use the baby changing countertop for leverage and after propping a foot against it, the shoe relents.

She's disappointed I'm not commiserating with her and she makes an assumption, "So you *like* to fly. Well, *I don't,* and that flight was awful. And the *landing,* I can't even talk about that part."

With one shoe off and one shoe on, I haul ass leaving her to ponder the question, "Was it the pilot's first landing, or was he drunk?"

The interior side of the terminal feeling almost *giddy.* I'm not sure what's making me happiest—the fact I didn't notice an iota of turbulence, or, that she didn't smell my feet and kick my ass.

I aggressively force the other sausage into the remaining shoe-sewer and head off to baggage claim. I have to take a series of escalators to get there so I put the earbuds back in and Adele continues,

"I'd go hungry,
I'd go black and blue.
I'd go crawling down the avenue.
There is nothing I wouldn't do,
To make you feel my love."

I'm flowing along on a horizontal steel staircase when it hits me—Brad and Emma are close. If Brad received the text I sent him via Kelly in Detroit, my dinner will play off an *offensively* large filet mignon, medium rare, drowning in béarnaise sauce. There'll be grilled asparagus, twice baked potato, and a salad celebrating every fresh vegetable in the grocery store.

And oh yeah, while I'm at it, I'm gonna get my drink on. I'm gonna drink the hell out of some water. But not water that I'm schlepping in a camelbak, or having to carry in a plastic bottle. And not water that's been boiled in a pot, and not water that flirts dangerously with lethal bacteria.

I'll never take water for granted again. There are many, many things I'll never take for granted again.

I'm ready to dance, but I'm not wearing rose colored glasses. I know life can be brutal. I know the dance floor gets closed periodically for waxing. Learn another lesson, dance a little more. Here comes another one, ouch—dance like a mofo in *this* minute.

I don't know how many more day's I'll get on this earth, but on the day God calls me home, or, a random buzzard draws my number, I want to know I did the best I could, for as many as I could, in love.

I'm starting to mainline adrenaline and begin to walk with purpose on the escalator. Now that *I'm* walking, I want everyone who isn't, to *stay to the right*.

I'm not sure of the physics and the *math*, but the increase in speed also increases the inertia, so stepping on and off the escalators, jars and hurts my knees. *Jesus, please just get me to baggage claim.* I'm back to Adele, and she's now emphatic,

"I've known it from the moment that we met, no doubt in my mind where you belong."

At this point, her soul is the choirmaster –
" ...the winds of change are blowing wild and free;
 you ain't seen nothin' like me yet."

I remove the earbuds and drape the cord around my neck.

The final escalator is the one to baggage claim and it moves up and down. As soon as I step on it I notice the nicely dressed man in a dark gray suit a few steps below me. When I catch up to him I get distracted by the thought, "He looks so clean. I bet he smells good too."

I bend down to see if I can get a whiff of his cologne, but more importantly, a view of the bottom of the escalator. I can't see below the slanted ceiling yet, so I pre-console myself with the thought, "Oh well, I doubt anyone will be here anyway. Brad always picks me up at the curb outside of baggage claim, and Emma's probably at work."

I bend over again to check but because my backpack is draped on a single shoulder, it shifts forward and lands right on top of the sharp dressed man. It makes a loud "oomph" sound that triggers a laugh. I try to cover with a cough, followed closely with a sincere apology, "I'm so sorry. Excuse me please." He's gracious and helps me pass. I want to say *Dhanyabad*, but I say thank you instead. Adele promises, "There is nothing I wouldn't do, to make you feel my love." and see long red hair framing a poster, "Welcome home, Mama! I'm so proud of you!"

Then I see a larger set of hands holding a ton of roses and another welcome home poster. Their reactions are identical. Both reverberating with relief. It's as if they weren't sure they'd ever see me alive again. I'm getting the message they missed me too.

With the landing site engaged, I take advantage of forward motion and lunge off the last steps into arms; arms that pull me in, and out of the way of creating a human pile-up.

The universe is telling me—no, it's *singing* to me— **"Move on, do you, and *every day, dance fearlessly!*"**

The irony stretches into humor as I realize, the most powerful lesson I've ever learned, was taught by …

*a random buzzard in Kathmandu.*

# ~The End~

# About the Author

**Suzanne Link, MA, LPC**

A native of Tuscaloosa, Alabama, Suzanne has lived in Charlotte, NC since 1986. She has been a psychotherapist in private practice for over 20 years. In 2009 she went through cancer and in 2012 she went through the high Himalaya. Cancer changed her life, Nepal changed her!

To learn more about opportunities to have Suzanne speak to your group visit www.arandombuzzard.com

# From the bottom of my heart...

**Thank you Mary Gottschalk.** Without you, *A Random Buzzard in Kathmandu* probably wouldn't be here. You spent countless hours teaching and helping me believe, then you devoted endless hours to editing. There aren't enough ways to say *thank you*, and words are insufficient to express my love and respect for you.

Mary works as a freelance writer, ghost writer, and editor. She's written two books including her memoir, *Sailing Down the Moonbeam*, and a novel, *A Fitting Place*. Contact Mary at www.marycgottschalk.com

**Thank you Charlie Wittmack, Esq.** Whether it was Divine intervention or serendipity that brought our paths together, meeting you was a game changer for me. You brought me into a world with unlimited possibilities. Thank you for challenging and inspiring me. www.theworldtri.com  www.ESPN.go.com.

With Charlie Wittmack, October, 2013
Above + Beyond Cancer's Night of Inspiration
Des Moines, Iowa

**Thank you Dr. Richard Deming, M.D.** You role-model compassion, patience, love, and kindness. You bring out the best in others and you make me want to be a better person!
www.aboveandbeyondcancer.org

**Thank you Brad Link, Emma Cooke, and Martha Berry.** You supported and believed in me when I needed it the most. However, you also made some *shady* calls that could have back-fired big time. But we know, I would have called it exactly the same way. You're great armchair quarterbacks, or, you're lucky as hell; either way, I'm glad you're on my team. I love you guys

Emma and Me on her college graduation weekend – May 2017

**Thank you Above and Beyond Cancer, Imja Tse Family.** Every person on the trip played a part in creating an experience beyond my wildest dreams! Thank you for embracing me, crusty boogers and all.

**Thank you John Richard.** Your photos and videos are almost as amazing as you! Thank you for sharing this gift. www.bocceballfilms.com

**Thank you Asian Trekking Staff.** As Guardian Angels of the High Himalaya, our journey was made because of you.

My hearts greatest gratitude goes to *my* Tensing, *my brother*.

**Thank you to my Mom and step Dad, Sue and Arnold Mills.** You taught me to be strong and independent, and while we haven't always seen eye to eye, the strongest and best parts of me, come from you.

**Thank you Pamela Pearce.** Your support and mentoring were invaluable. Now go and finish your Great American Novel!